RESS Essentials

A practical introduction to programming responsive websites using an innovative methodology in web design and development

Joanna Krenz- Kurowska

Jerzy Kurowski

BIRMINGHAM - MUMBAI

RESS Essentials

First published: October 2013

Production Reference: 1181013

Published by Packt Publishing Ltd.
Livery Place
35 Livery Street
Birmingham B3 2PB, UK.

ISBN 978-1-84969-694-4

www.packtpub.com

Cover Image by Joanna Krenz-Kurowska (23dragons.com)

Credits

Authors

Joanna Krenz-Kurowska

Jerzy Kurowski

Reviewers

Arley McBlain

Marc Pàmpols

Acquisition Editors

Martin Bell

Gregory Wild

Commissioning Editor

Sruthi Kutty

Technical Editors

Gauri Dasgupta

Failsal Siddiqui

Copy Editors

Brandt D'Mello

Gladson Monteiro

Lavina Pereira

Adithi Shetty

Project Coordinator

Amigya Khurana

Proofreader

Sandra Hopper

Indexers

Mariammal Chettiyar

Priya Subramani

Production Coordinator

Pooja Chiplunkar

Cover Work

Pooja Chiplunkar

About the Authors

Joanna Krenz-Kurowska has been working as a freelance graphic designer and web designer for 12 years. She lives in the mountains on the south-west of Poland. She spent the last few years working for clients on five continents, blogging about web design and technology for the 99designs community blog, winning dozens of web design contests and following her passions: art photography, running marathons, and graphic arts. She is a member of the art union New Mill Artists' Colony. Teaming up with Jerzy Kurowski, she creates complete digital products like websites or multimedia programs. She loves challenges like swimming in ice air holes, long-distance mountain running, or exploring new areas in web design. You can learn more about her on www.23dragons.com.

Jerzy Kurowski, after graduating from the Academy of Fine Arts in Krakow in 1993, became interested in computer graphics. At that time he primarily designed for print but simultaneously he learned authoring and programing multimedia. In 1998, he started to create products for the Internet, and overtime freelance web development gradually became his main source of income. Having worked with a plethora of technologies in his life, today he tries to focus on developing the engaging user web interfaces with the use of PHP, AS3, JS, CSS, and HTML. When he is not coding or designing, he lives a highlander's life in the Giant Mountains on the Polish-Czech border in Central Europe. Follow him on https://twitter.com/JerzyKurowski.

About the Reviewers

Arley McBlain is a Lead Front End Developer at the Canadian web agency, `Thrillworks Inc.`, and works with many notable clients including BlackBerry, Tim Hortons, and Suncor. Arley has been making websites for over 18 years with experience in many roles; but he is now focusing on responsive and mobile-friendly frontend development.

Arley's passion for this industry has him active on social media outlets, forums, and occasionally writing for web blogs like CSS Tricks, Six Revisions, and Web Design Depot. He blogs at `arleym.com` and tweets as `@ArleyM`.

Marc Pàmpols is a tech entrepreneur, developer, analyst, and project leader from Spain. He started working at a couple of small development companies for three years. Later he founded `YoteConozco.com`, a Spanish dating social network that reached more than 50,000 users.

From 2007 until today, he is working at an IT company (Semic S.A.), leading the development of Python and Plone websites for privately held companies and public administration. Marc has worked for clients, such as the Spanish Ministry of Culture, Government of Andorra, and Tarragona, Vic, and Cambrils City Councils. He always had a strong interest in both frontend and backend development.

> I would like to thank my mum, dad, dog, co-workers, and my friends at bixo demoscene group for protecting me during the review of this book.

www.PacktPub.com

Support files, eBooks, discount offers and more

You might want to visit www.PacktPub.com for support files and downloads related to your book.

Did you know that Packt offers eBook versions of every book published, with PDF and ePub files available? You can upgrade to the eBook version at www.PacktPub.com and as a print book customer, you are entitled to a discount on the eBook copy. Get in touch with us at service@packtpub.com for more details.

At www.PacktPub.com, you can also read a collection of free technical articles, sign up for a range of free newsletters and receive exclusive discounts and offers on Packt books and eBooks.

http://PacktLib.PacktPub.com

Do you need instant solutions to your IT questions? PacktLib is Packt's online digital book library. Here, you can access, read and search across Packt's entire library of books.

Why Subscribe?

- Fully searchable across every book published by Packt
- Copy and paste, print and bookmark content
- On demand and accessible via web browser

Free Access for Packt account holders

If you have an account with Packt at www.PacktPub.com, you can use this to access PacktLib today and view nine entirely free books. Simply use your login credentials for immediate access.

Table of Contents

Preface

RESS is a new methodology in the world of web design and development. It attempts to solve the problems that accompany the **Responsive Web Design (RWD)** approach to web design. RESS is still in its infancy, but it is growing at an exponential rate.

RESS Essentials shows you how to make server-side applications smarter and more aware of a visitor's environment limitations (device, screen size, and browser). This allows you to create faster and more reliable websites. Through this book, you will build a solid base of knowledge on RESS-related technologies, while the step-by-step tutorials will help you to create your own RESS system.

This book is an introduction to the RESS alchemy and gives you an incentive to build your own RESS lab. It will give you a broad overview of the multiple techniques used to code responsive websites in responsible ways. Beginning with an overview of RWD, you will learn the steps involved in setting up RWD for client-side development. You will then learn how to scale images using client and server-side technology. By the end of this book, you will have learned about the implementation of RESS application patterns, browser feature detection, and various RESS architectures. This book will also teach you how to use jQuery with some RWD design patterns and how to employ REST API for RWD pages.

What this book covers

Chapter 1, Why Does RWD Change the Internet?, is a brief description of Responsive Web Design history, its benefits, and the controversies it caused among web developers. It also gives a brief introduction to RESS.

Chapter 2, Sample RWD Setup for Client-Side Development, describes creating a sample responsive HTML document with the help of Twitter's Bootstrap framework and Gridpak tool.

Chapter 3, Server Side Setup – Device Detection Libraries, covers using WURF (OnSite and Cloud versions) and Dave Olsen's Detector library to detect device features.

Chapter 4, Sample RESS Page, explains four complete RESS solutions to get a device's information that can be used to build an appropriate version of an HTML document within server-side application.

Chapter 5, Responsive Images Client- and Server-Side Approaches, talks about several ways to deliver resolution-dependent images, such as the script from `adaptive-images.com`, the `<picture>` element polyfill, or the RESS solution from the previous chapter.

Chapter 6, Performance, explains optimization strategies and useful tools.

Chapter 7, Extending with jQuery, starts by integrating the Twitter Bootstrap carousel component with our RESS test system. Next it covers creating the jQuery plugin from scratch to make the table responsive by converting it into an accordion component below the screen width defined with the media query.

Chapter 8, Employing a REST API for RWD, explains how to create a REST API with a Slim PHP framework and an AJAX application integrated with our RESS module, which we created before.

What you need for this book

To run some examples from this book you need to have some kind of AMP (Apache, mySQL, PHP) environment. For those using Windows, the easiest way to go is to use the WAMP server in the default configuration. Links to the respective packages for other systems can be found at `http://en.wikipedia.org/wiki/List_of_Apache-MySQL-PHP_packages`.

Who this book is for

This book is aimed primarily at web developers interested in writing applications that leverage both client-and server-side code to optimize content for various devices.

Conventions

In this book, you will find a number of styles of text that distinguish between different kinds of information. Here are some examples of these styles, and an explanation of their meaning.

Code words in text are shown as follows: "We can include other contexts through the use of the `include` directive."

A block of code is set as follows:

```
<picture alt="">
  <source media="(min-width: 45em)"
    srcset="large-1.jpg 1x, large-2.jpg 2x">
  <source media="(min-width: 18em)"
    srcset="med-1.jpg 1x, med-2.jpg 2x">
  <source srcset="small-1.jpg 1x, small-2.jpg 2x">
  <img src="small-1.jpg">
</picture>
```

New terms and **important words** are shown in bold. Words that you see on the screen, in menus or dialog boxes for example, appear in the text like this: "In the **JavaScript components** section, do not select any checkbox."

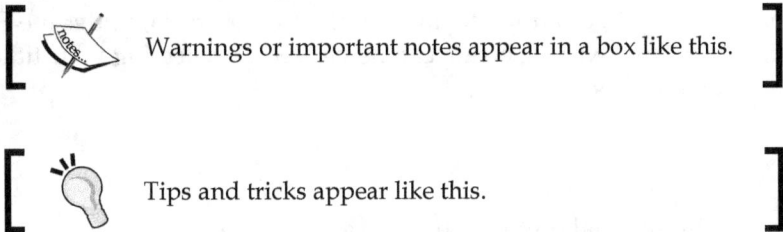

Warnings or important notes appear in a box like this.

Tips and tricks appear like this.

Reader feedback

Feedback from our readers is always welcome. Let us know what you think about this book—what you liked or may have disliked. Reader feedback is important for us to develop titles that you really get the most out of.

To send us general feedback, simply send an e-mail to `feedback@packtpub.com`, and mention the book title via the subject of your message.

If there is a topic that you have expertise in and you are interested in either writing or contributing to a book, see our author guide on `www.packtpub.com/authors`.

Customer support

Now that you are the proud owner of a Packt book, we have a number of things to help you to get the most from your purchase.

Downloading the example code

You can download the example code files for all Packt books you have purchased from your account at http://www.packtpub.com. If you purchased this book elsewhere, you can visit http://www.packtpub.com/support and register to have the files e-mailed directly to you.

Errata

Although we have taken every care to ensure the accuracy of our content, mistakes do happen. If you find a mistake in one of our books—maybe a mistake in the text or the code—we would be grateful if you would report this to us. By doing so, you can save other readers from frustration and help us improve subsequent versions of this book. If you find any errata, please report them by visiting http://www.packtpub.com/submit-errata, selecting your book, clicking on the **errata submission form** link, and entering the details of your errata. Once your errata are verified, your submission will be accepted and the errata will be uploaded on our website, or added to any list of existing errata, under the Errata section of that title. Any existing errata can be viewed by selecting your title from http://www.packtpub.com/support.

Piracy

Piracy of copyright material on the Internet is an ongoing problem across all media. At Packt, we take the protection of our copyright and licenses very seriously. If you come across any illegal copies of our works, in any form, on the Internet, please provide us with the location address or website name immediately so that we can pursue a remedy.

Please contact us at copyright@packtpub.com with a link to the suspected pirated material.

We appreciate your help in protecting our authors, and our ability to bring you valuable content.

Questions

You can contact us at questions@packtpub.com if you are having a problem with any aspect of the book, and we will do our best to address it.

1
Why Does RWD Change the Internet?

This book is about two phenomena in the world of contemporary web design and web development, RWD and RESS. RWD stands for Responsive Web Design and RESS means RWD with Server Side Components. Both are based on attempts to find a way to deliver content to multiple devices more easily, and efficiently while reducing development time and keeping application and data structures maintainable. The RWD concept appeared first in 2010 in an article by *Ethan Marcotte* (available at `http://alistapart.com/article/responsive-web-design`). He presented an approach that allows us to progressively enhance page design within different viewing contexts with the help of fluid grids, flexible images, and media queries. This approach was opposed to the one that separates websites geared toward specific devices. Instead of two or more websites (desktop and mobile), we could have one that adapts to all devices. The technical foundation of RWD (as proposed in Marcotte's article) consists of three things, fluid grids, flexible images, and media queries.

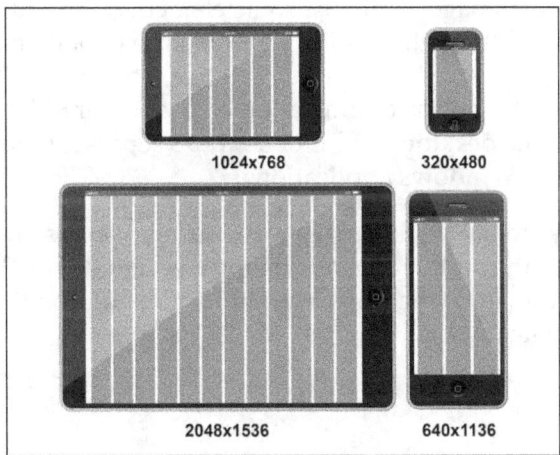

Illustration: Fluid (and responsive) grid adapts to device using both column width and column count

Fluid grid is basically nothing more than a concept of dividing the monitor width into modular columns, often accompanied by some kind of a CSS framework (some of the best-known examples were the 960 grid system, blueprint, pure, 1140px grid, and elastic), that is, a base stylesheet that simplifies and standardizes writing website-specific CSS. What makes it fluid is the use of relative measurements like %, em, or rem. With changing the screen (or the window), the number of these columns changes (thanks to CSS statements enclosed in media queries). This allows us to adjust the design layout to device capabilities (screen width and pixel density in particular).

Images in such a layout become fluid by using a simple technique of setting width, x% or max-width, 100% in CSS, which causes the image to scale proportionally.

With those two methods and a little help from media queries, one can radically change the page layout and handle this enormous, up to 800 percent, difference between the thinnest and the widest screen (WQXGA's 2560px/iPhone's 320px). This is a big step forward and a good base to start creating One Web, that is, to use one URL to deliver content to all the devices. Unfortunately, that is not enough to achieve results that would provide an equally great experience and fast loading websites for everybody.

The RESS idea

Besides screen width, we may need to take into account other things such as bandwidth and pay-per-bandwidth plans, processor speed, available memory, level of HTML/CSS compatibility, monitoring color depth, and possible navigation methods (touch screen, buttons, and keyboard). On a practical level, it means we may have to optimize images and navigation patterns, and reduce page complexity for some devices. To make this possible, some Server Side solutions need to be engaged. We may use Server Side just for optimizing images. Server Side optimization lets us send pages with just some elements adjusted or a completely changed page; we can rethink the application structure to build a RESTful web interface and turn our Server Side application into a web service. The more we need to place responsibility for device optimization on the Server Side, the closer we get to the old way of disparate desktops and mobile web's separate mobile domains, such as iPhone, Android, or Windows applications.

There are many ways to build responsive websites but there is no golden rule to tell you which way is the best. It depends on the target audience, technical contexts, money, and time. Ultimately, the way to be chosen depends on the business decisions of the website owner.

When we decide to employ Server Side logic to optimize components of a web page designed in a responsive way, we are going the **RESS (Responsive Web Design with Server Side components)** way. RESS was proposed by Luke Wroblewski on his blog as a result of his experiences on extending RWD with Server Side components. Essentially, the idea was based on storing IDs of resources (such as images) and serving different versions of the same resource, optimized for some defined classes of devices. Device detection and assigning them to respective classes can be based on libraries such as WURFL or YABFDL.

Controversies

It is worth noting that both of these approaches raised many controversies. Introducing RWD has broken some long-established rules or habits such as standard screen width (the famous 960px maximum page width limit). It has put in question the long-practiced ways of dealing with mobile web (such as separate desktop and mobile websites). It is no surprise that it raises both delight and rage. One can easily find people calling this fool's gold, useless, too difficult, a fad, amazing, future proof, and so on. Each of those opinions has a reason behind it, for better or worse.

A glimpse of the following opinions may help us understand some of the key benefits and issues related to RWD.

"Separate mobile websites are a good thing"

You may have heard this line in an article by *Jason Grigsby*, *Css media query for mobile is fool's gold*, available at `http://blog.cloudfour.com/css-media-query-for-mobile-is-fools-gold/`.

Separate mobile websites allow reduction of bandwidth, prepare pages that are less CPU and memory intensive, and at the same time allow us to use some mobile-only features such as geolocation. Also, not all mobile browsers are wise enough to understand media queries.

That is generally true and media queries are not enough in most scenarios, but with some JavaScript (*Peter-Paul Koch* blog available at, `http://www.quirksmode.org/blog/archives/2010/08/combining_media.html#more`, describes a method to exclude some page elements or change the page structure via JS paired with media queries), it is possible to overcome many of those problems. At the same time, making a separate mobile website introduces its own problems and requires significant additional investment that can easily get to tens or hundreds of times more than the RWD solution (detecting devices, changing application logic, writing separate templates, integrating, and testing the whole thing). Also, at the end of the day, your visitors may prefer the mobile version, but this doesn't have to be the case. Users are often accessing the same content via various devices and providing consistent experience across all of them becomes more and more important.

The preceding controversy is just a part of a wider discussion on channels to provide content on the Internet. RWD and RESS are relatively new kids on the block. For years, technologies to provide content for mobile devices were being built and used, from device-detection libraries to platform-specific applications (such as iStore, Google Play, and MS). When, in 2010, US smartphone users started to spend more time using their mobile apps than browsers (*Mobile App Usage Further Dominates Web, Spurred by Facebook*, at `http://blog.flurry.com/bid/80241/Mobile-App-Usage-Further-Dominates-Web-Spurred-by-Facebook`), some hailed it as dangerous for the Web (*Apps: The Web Is The Platform*, available at `http://blog.mozilla.org/webdev/2012/09/14/apps-the-web-is-the-platform/`). A closer look at stats reveals though, that most of this time was spent on playing games. No matter how much time kids can spend playing Angry Birds now, after more than two years from then, people still prefer to read the news via a browser rather than via native mobile applications. The *Future of Mobile News* report from October 2012 reveals that for accessing news, 61 percent mobile users prefer a browser while 28 percent would rather use apps (*Future of Mobile News*, `http://www.journalism.org/analysis_report/future_mobile_news`). The British government is not keen on apps either, as they say, "Our position is that native apps are rarely justified" (UK Digital Cabinet Office blog, at `http://digital.cabinetoffice.gov.uk/2013/03/12/were-not-appy-not-appy-at-all/`).

Recently, Tim Berners-Lee, the inventor of the Web, criticized closed world apps such as those released by Apple for threatening openness and universality that the architects of the Internet saw as central to its design. He explains it the following way, "When you make a link, you can link to anything. That means people must be able to put anything on the Web, no matter what computer they have, what software they use, or which human language they speak and regardless of whether they have a wired or a wireless Internet connection." This kind of thinking goes in line with the RWD/RESS philosophy to have one URL for the same content, no matter what way you'd like to access it. Nonetheless, it is just one of the reasons why RWD became so popular during the last year.

"RWD is too difficult"

CSS coupled with JS can get really complex (some would say messy) and requires a lot of testing on all target browsers/platforms.

That is or was true. Building RWD websites requires good CSS knowledge and some battlefield experience in this field. But hey, learning is the most important skill in this industry. It actually gets easier and easier with new tools released nearly every week.

"RWD means degrading design"

Fluid layouts break the composition of the page; Mobile First and Progressive Enhancement mean, in fact, reducing design to a few simplistic and naive patterns.

 Actually the Mobile First concept contains two concepts. One is design direction and the second is the structure of CSS stylesheets, in particular the order of media queries.

With regard to design direction, the Mobile First concept is meant to describe the sequence of designs. First the design for a mobile should be created and then for a desktop. While there are several good reasons for using this approach, one should never forget the basic truth that at the end of the day only the quality of designs matters, not the order they were created in.

With regard to the stylesheet structure, Mobile First means that we first write statements for small screens and then add statements for wider screens, such as `@media screen and (min-width: 480px)`. It is a design principle meant to simplify the whole thing. It is assumed here that CSS for small screens is the simplest version, which will be progressively enhanced for larger screens. The idea is smart and helps to maintain a well-structured CSS but sometimes the opposite, the Desktop First approach, seems natural. Typical examples are tables with many columns. The Mobile First principle is not a religious dogma and should not be treated as such. As a side note, it remains an open question why this is still named Mobile First, while the new iPad-related statements should come here at the end (`min-width: 2000px`).

There are some examples of rather poor designs made by RWD celebrities. But there are also examples of great designs that happened, thanks to the freedom that RWD gave to the web design world.

The rapid increase in Internet access via mobile devices during 2012 made RWD one of the hottest topics in web design. The numbers vary across countries and websites but no matter what numbers you look at, one thing is certain, mobile is already big and will soon get even bigger (valuable stats on mobile use are available at http://www.thinkwithgoogle.com/mobileplanet/en/). Statistics are not the only reason why Responsive Web Design became popular. Equally important are the benefits for web designers, users, website owners, and developers.

RWD benefits

Let's take a look at the advantages RWD and RESS can offer to members of each of their various user groups.

Freedom for designers

RWD for designers means the end of the standard-screen-width paradigm that ruled the Web for a long time. When I started web designing, standard screen width was considered to be 600px. Soon it reached 800px and stabilized for years at 1024px (960px standard available width for design).

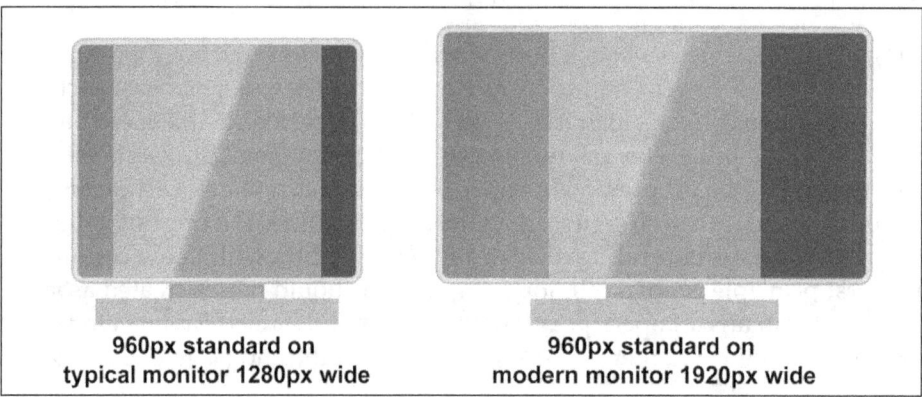

960px standard on
typical monitor 1280px wide

960px standard on
modern monitor 1920px wide

Illustration – standard screen width

Following this "standard", the lowest screen width our visitors used to have, resulted in designs using only 50-75 percent of the screen real estate that most monitors could provide. The rest usually just had some nice background pattern.

Responsive Web Design that had to adjust to various devices' resolutions made the "standard width" concept obsolete. If we do responsive design, why not use all the available space? Standard document 960px width uses less than 40% screen real estate on a monitor more than 2500px wide. Creating documents that use 100% available width allows us to create more engaging and interesting designs. Browsing the best web designs of 2012, one gets the impression that someone opened a box with fullscreen website designs that provide a cinematic or game-like experience (you can see that most of them provide fullscreen experience). This is just the beginning.

Invest less, reach out to a larger audience

This is probably the dream of any website owner. RWD or RESS is not a silver bullet against all problems to provide content to devices. Each case should be carefully analyzed to find out what type of solution is best, or at least possible, in a particular circumstance. Having said that, in many typical applications it is the cheapest and the fastest way to web design. Additional costs of design, implementation, and testing will probably not be even comparable with the cost of creating several mobile website versions together with respective native applications (hybrid applications as described at `http://www.wired.com/insights/2012/11/native-apps-vs-mobile-web/`).

The Web is a good thing for users, and they definitely prefer a browsable website over one they can hardly see on their smartphone/tablet.

Ability to link content is crucial for the Internet. Users expect links to work no matter how they access the Internet, and it is not possible to link to content inside some native apps. Browsing a mobile version of a website with desktop browsers or the opposite is not comfortable. It may happen though as a natural consequence of the nature of links.

Lowering budget constraint means that more websites can afford to optimize content for more devices, which will hopefully make the Web easier to browse on smartphones.

Users

It is hard to find statistics on how much consumers like or dislike responsive layouts. They don't care much about the technology involved. For them, experience is the only thing that matters. RESS is an approach, one of many, that may help in providing great experiences across devices. Of course it is important to provide this experience, instead of failing before we provide anything or providing unusable content. Whenever conversion of an existing website to responsive layout is considered, we need to understand the limitations and, when possible, overcome them with the use of Server Side components and JavaScript.

After we are able to provide the user experiences we intended with our design, the benefits are obvious, which are as follows:

- On big screens, the web page finally uses the whole possible area, which enables a more engaging experience.
- On small screens, readability is guaranteed.
- Lowering costs of "going mobile" for website owners means that users will get more websites optimized for devices than it would be possible without RWD.
- Bandwidth issues can be solved with RESS.
- In many scenarios native applications or mobile websites can provide better a user experience, but before resigning from responsive solutions some questions should be asked such as, does this advantage justify the difference in the cost of development and maintaining separate versions of the website? Is our device detection kit really as reliable as we'd like to believe? And how future proof will this solution be? Borders between device classes (used to determine templates to device relations) are blurry and will fade even more with time.

Future proof is a buzzword often used by the RWD community as a selling point for RWD: www.techopedia.com states; in reality, very few things are truly future proof and that is the sad truth about all web things. RWD probably will be more future proof than native applications; the future will tell us. Nonetheless, it will be definitely cheaper to maintain RWD/RESS websites than native applications.

Developers

Most RWD critics come from the developers' community. This is surprising, but not very. Multiresolution design complexity adds to an everlasting tension between designers and developers. Implementing what the designer created in Photoshop is often a challenge for programmers, even without the necessity to make it fluidic and responsive. Besides that, RWD is a concept with no API or technical documentation to study. It introduces many problems, enough to mention responsive (adapting to resolution) images. The good news is that after two years of evolution we have some well-tested CSS frameworks, a growing number of JS libraries, and last but not least, responsive design principles, which are implemented in new versions of popular open-source content management platforms such as Drupal. In Drupal 8 there are several responsive elements. One of them is the Picture display formatter for image fields, being a Drupal way to implement the `picture` element proposal for HTML5, available at `http://picture.responsiveimages.org/`.

On the list of tools a responsive design developer may need, `respond.js` (available at `https://github.com/scottjehl/Respond`) takes first place, a lightweight script that enables responsive design in browsers that don't support CSS3 media queries.

If you need a conditional resource, loading another JavaScript `Modernizr` (available at `http://modernizr.com/`) can help you.

There are many responsive Boilerplates to help you get started quickly. HTML5 Boilerplate (available at `www.html5boilerplate.com`) is most often used and can be used as a starting point for almost every web project. It contains an HTML template with `normalize.css` that normalizes default stylesheets of various browsers, `Modernizr` script, and examples of best-practice server configuration files.

The base version is not a responsive CSS framework, as it doesn't impose on the developer any particular way to handle responsiveness, but you can also get it in two other flavors, Responsive or Bootstrap. Each of them proposes its own perspective on building the page structure. Responsive is a concept of three views and layout versions, mobile, intermediate, and large.

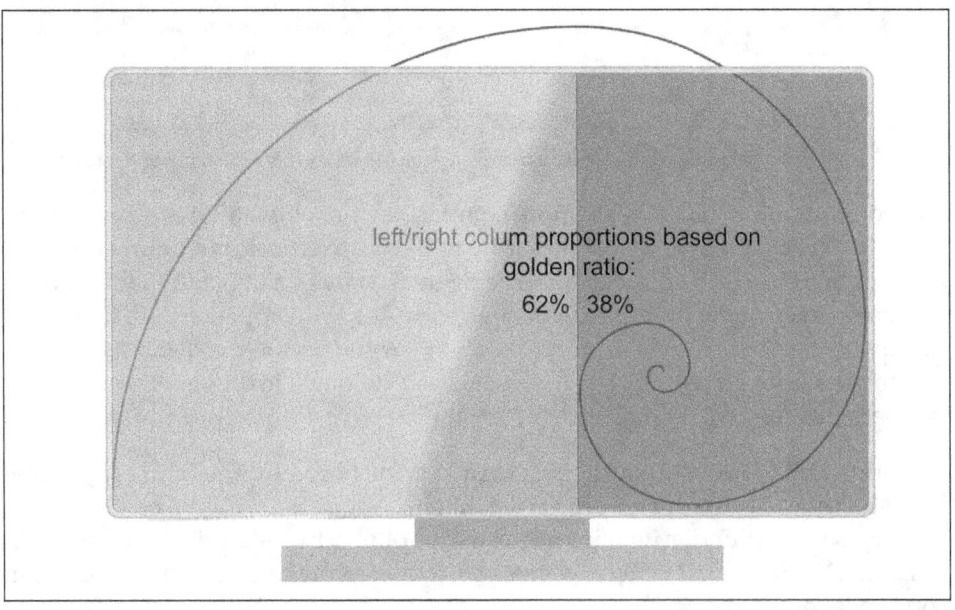

left/right colum proportions based on golden ratio:
62% 38%

HTML5 Boilerplate Responsive features two columns and typographic settings optimized for readability

It is perfect for fast, simple projects that don't require a complex layout.

The Bootstrap version is a responsive framework based on a 12-column responsive grid. The 12-column internal structure of this version (and its possible applications) is explained in detail at http://getbootstrap.com/css/.

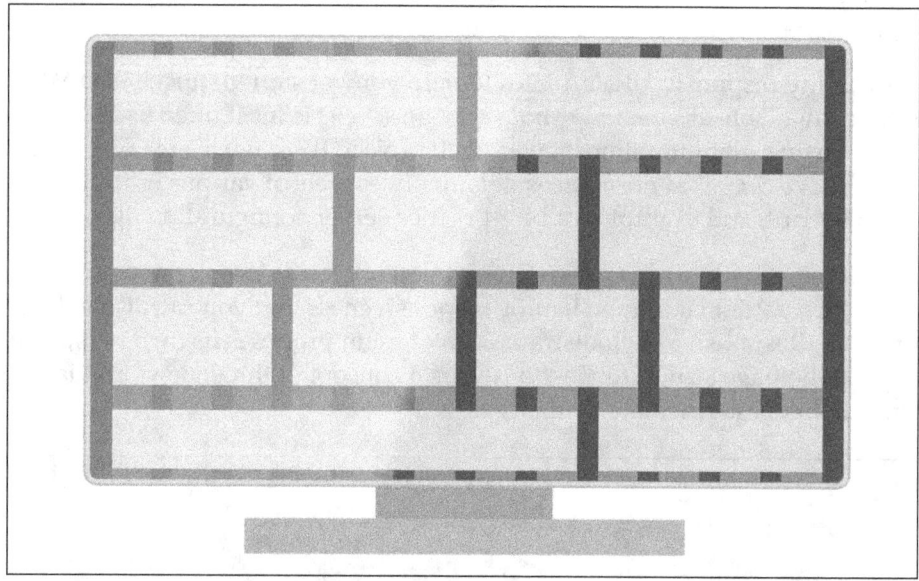

12 columns of default grid in HTML5 Boilerplate give some flexibility in planning the page

Twelve columns allow us to create more complex layouts, but still it is a rather rigid system. Most designers would not be happy to have a fixed column number, with widths and margins defined for them. During the last five years, many tools and frameworks aimed at creating all kinds of grids on the Web appeared; ZURB CSS Grid Builder available at http://www.zurb.com/playground/css-grid-builder and Gridulator available at http://gridulator.com/ to name just two. A more extensive list can be found at http://www.thegridsystem.org/categories/tools/.

As flexibility and speed in creating responsive grids becomes one of the key issues in the web design / web development workflow, Adobe is trying its best to keep this market segment under its wings. It is hard not to admit that their tools lead the race. Inside Dreamweaver CS6 one can use a two-step process to streamline, creating responsive layouts.

At the first step it is possible to set up grids for three resolutions, with any number of columns on each screen width.

On the created framework, one can place content blocks and adjust their placement for each of three screen resolutions by dragging their edges.

Generated code is based on HTML5 Boilerplate and can be manually tweaked. The Dreamweaver interface allows us to also build content blocks on a grid framework.

On 14 February 2013 Adobe released the public preview of a completely new tool: Edge Reflow (free at the time of writing this). Its sole purpose is to allow fast and easy creation of CSS and HTML for responsive layouts.

RWD evolution and experiments

Originally RWD consisted of three basic technologies used in a somewhat defined way, shown as follows:

- **Fluid grids**: Based on % measurements
- **Flexible images**: Scaled down with the CSS max-width trick
- **Media queries made with philosophy Mobile First or Progressive Enhancement**: That means code for the smallest screen was written first and then features for larger screens were added

The most important additions are the `Modernizr` and `Respond.js` libraries used in conjunction with a number of techniques to improve cross-browser compatibility.

Fluid grids should rather be named fluid and responsive in the original version. What is the difference? A fluid grid works like an old-fashioned fluid layout, that is, the columns' widths change when the browser window's width changes. A responsive grid responds to this change by changing the number of columns. In the original orthodox RWD concept, grids did both and the change was driven together by media queries and by the use of percentage values to set up layout.

For some people and projects this approach worked well but:

- Some were not happy with fluid columns and made "frameless grids" (available at `http://framelessgrid.com/`), a CSS grid system with columns of fixed width
- Some decided that it's better to use `em` or `rem` based scaling to take the resolution out of the equation and made The Goldilocks Approach an HTML and CSS Boilerplate (available at `http://goldilocksapproach.com/`)
- Some thought that breaking a grid into bricks instead of columns may be more funny and made Masonry (available at `http://masonry.desandro.com/`)
- Some (authors of this book among them) are happy to write their media queries by hand and adjust layout when it is necessary in a way required by the design

Last but not least RESS techniques emerged. Nobody really defined how RESS is supposed to work, besides that it couples RWD with Server Side components. A neat example of this kind of thinking is Adaptive Images (available at `http://adaptive-images.com/`), the PHP library that takes care of resizing images on the server. A similar solution was employed at Boston Globe, the huge news website being the flagship example of a complex RWD implementation.

Summary

The RESS idea can be described as Server Side optimizing page components for devices with the use of browser-features detection. In other words, RESS is an attempt to marry client-side responsive design achieved by using media queries and some JavaScript with Server Side logic. The purpose here is to make the whole system more efficient, and to overcome the constraints of a client-side application. These are vague statements and we need to be more precise before we can build any actual RESS systems. To know what RESS can do for us we have to know what problems we need to address and what Server Side infrastructure we have in place. RESS solutions are most often employed just for image optimization, but you could use it for serving the 3D Web GL version for those who can use it, FLASH for those who have it, CSS animations for those who see it, and so on.

The most underestimated RWD advantage is that it allows us to make better designs: designs that always use all the available screen width. This is the case for the first time since the very beginning of the Internet. The old way of making fluid layouts was a flawed solution that never grew out of childhood diseases. In the following chapter, we will build a really simple RWD example based on the HTML5 Boilerplate, using a responsive navigation component from H5BP (HTML5 Boilerplate). We will not use the default grid system but replace it with one that we define ourselves with the Gridpak service.

2
Sample RWD Setup for Client-Side Development

To test and learn RWD and RESS concepts, we will build a demo website. In this chapter we are going to focus on client-side design and development. We will go through the process of implementing a simple design with practical application of RWD concepts such as fluid images, responsive grids, and media queries.

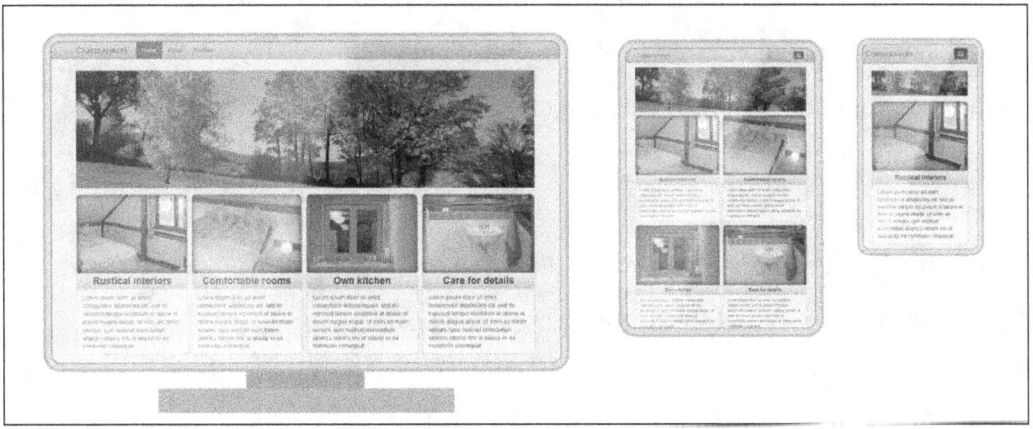

A sample responsive homepage design we are going to build in this chapter

During the process, we are going to look closer at HTML and CSS constructs often used to build responsive web pages. To implement our design, we will employ the often-used frontend framework, Twitter's Bootstrap, based on 12 fluid columns. We don't need most of its components (we are only going to use the responsive navigation bar), but we will seize the opportunity to get acquainted with this useful tool. Our design uses variable column count depending on the screen size. To achieve it, we may use the Gridpak tool, which lets us create complex variable column grids with an intuitive interface. Then we will learn how to integrate the two, the Gridpak grid and Bootstrap. Finally, we will add custom classes to format the document and fine tune the page look on various screen sizes by adjusting font sizes and fixing issues that might crop up.

Bootstrap custom compilation setup

To get a customized version of Twitter's Bootstrap, we go to `http://getbootstrap.com/customize/` where you can select which components you need and customize the LESS variables such as colors fonts. In the current version (3.0), the build script was improved and cleaned. Now it's easy to get a really lightweight setup. We just need basic styles and a responsive navigation bar. To get our custom build, first uncheck all the checkboxes. Then, in the **Common CSS** section, select the following checkbox:

- **Forms**: This is required by the `Navbar` component

In the **Components** section, select the following checkboxes:

- Navs
- Navbar

In the **JavaScript components** section, do not select any checkbox.

In the **Utilities** section, select the following checkboxes:

- Basic utilities
- Component animations (for JS)

Under the **jQuery plugins** header in the **Linked to components** section, do not select any checkbox.

Finally, in the **Magic** section, select the following checkboxes:

- Collapse
- Transitions (required for any kind of animation)

Let's also get a version of Bootstrap with grids. To do this, we have to check **Grid system** in the **Common CSS** section.

We override the Bootstrap color settings with our own styles, so you can skip the following color setup section, and on the bottom of the page find the **Compile and Download** button. Let's name this version `bootstrap_grid.zip`.

Testing the Bootstrap grid system

The downloaded files are ZIP archives containing two directories (**css** and **js**) and some files inside each of them. First we'd like to see and test the default Bootstrap's grid system. So let's extract the `bootstrap_grid.zip` contents to the `/assets/` subdirectory of our test website. I renamed the `boostrap.css` file inside the `css` directory to `boostrap_grid.css` and added `grids_visual.css` for styles necessary to visualize the grid in the browser. The file `bootstrap_grids.html` is an HTML document with markup describing a few rows of the Bootstrap grid system.

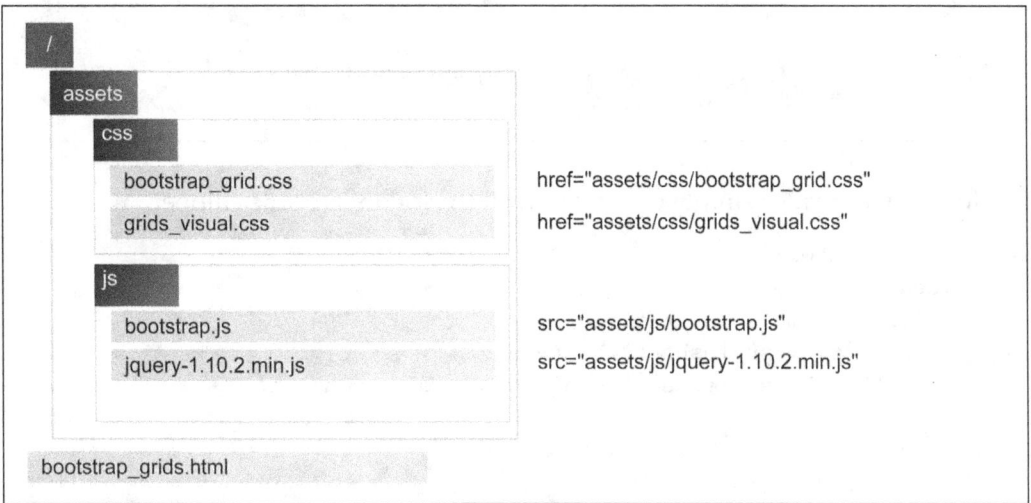

Files necessary to test Twitter's Bootstrap grids

The Bootstrap grid system consists of 12 columns that may be merged for some or all of its media queries defined for the following four stops:

- **Extra small**: For phones (<768px)
- **Small**: For tablets (≥768px)
- **Medium**: For desktops (≥992px)
- **Large**: For desktops (≥1200px)

It's worth noting that in this approach, everything smaller than 768 pixels is considered extra small.

Now we can create an HTML structure to preview and test Twitter's Bootstrap-responsive columns. In Version 3 of Twitter's Bootstrap, published in the middle of August 2013, several changes were introduced to allow more flexibility and simplify HTML at the same time.

The default 12-columns grid in Twitter's Bootstrap has fixed column count. Below 768px columns turn to rows in a one-column layout, as shown in the following figure:

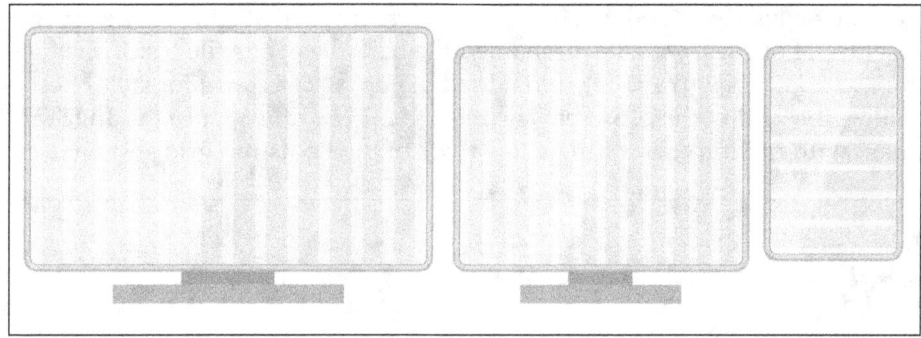

To do this, we create a simple document with the following code snippet:

```
<!DOCTYPE html>
  <head>
    <title>Sample grid</title>
    <link rel="stylesheet" href="css/bootstrap_grid.css">
    <link rel="stylesheet" href="css/grids_visual.css">
  </head>
  <body>
    <div class="row">
    <div class="col-md-1 magenta_bar"></div>
      [12 lines]
    <div class="col-md-1 magenta_bar"></div>
    </div>
```

The 12 rows in the code we just saw `<div class="col-md-1 magenta_bar"></div>` placed inside `<div class="row">` is a typical responsive row.

Class `col-md-1` means that the coloumn width of this `div` will be one in all the resolutions and will extend to fullscreen width below 768px. The next row in our document contains more complex formatting, shown as follows:

```
<div class="row">
  <div class="col-md-4 col-sm-5  col-xs-6 magenta_bar">
  </div>
  <div class="col-md-4 col-sm-2  col-xs-6 magenta_bar">
  </div>
  <div class="col-md-4 col-sm-5  col-xs-12 magenta_bar">
  </div>
</div>
</body>
</html>
```

Assigning three classes such as `col-md-4`, `col-sm-5`, and `col-xs-6` to our `div` column is explained as follows:

- `col-md-4` means that it is four columns wide (33 percent) on medium and bigger screens
- `col-sm-5` means that it is five columns wide (41.6667 percent) on small and bigger screens
- `col-xs-6` means that it is six columns wide (50 percent) on extra small and bigger screens

The media queries are written in the Mobile First order, which means that statements for larger screens override those for smaller ones.

The document structure can be seen in the following image:

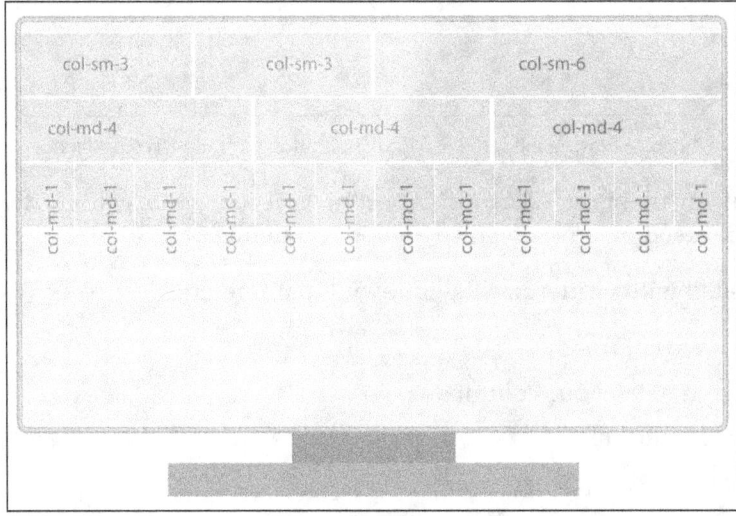

Integrating Gridpak

Flexibility of Twitter's Bootstrap grid system is improved in Version 3, but we will use a grid created with another grid-generation script; Gridpak (available at `http://gridpak.com/`) from Erskine Design is an amazing tool that allows us to create any grid for any media query stop with an intuitive interface. Its main features are as follows:

- Interactive creation of percent-based grids with variable column count
- Creating media query stops of any screen width

When you create a grid, you can download the following files:

- `.png` design templates for all the necessary steps
- `.js` script that draws the grid (the grid visibility can be turned on or off with the *g* key)
- `.css` file with media queries and grid columns (with column spans defined as `span_x` classes)
- `.less` and `.scss` files

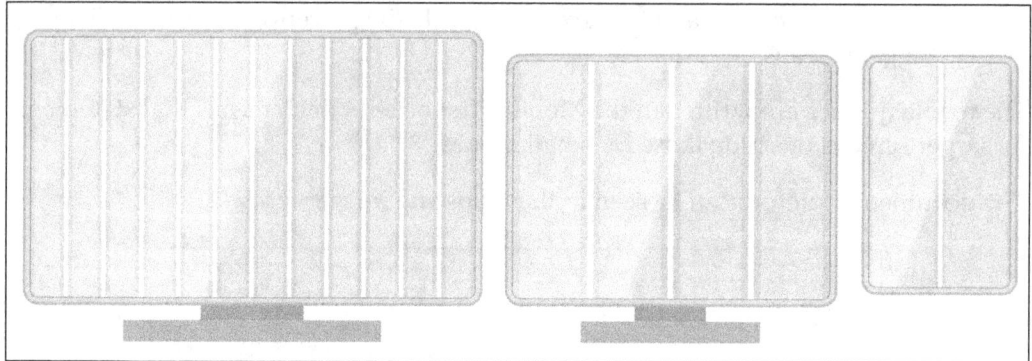

A demo showing the setup of a grid application with some typical blocks

With Gridpak (available at `www.gridpak.com`), you can create grids with variable column count based on any screen size steps you define.

Sample I created with Grider has the following parameters:

- **>320**: Two columns
- **320< and <799**: Four columns
- **800<**: 12 columns

The grid CSS from Gridpak is very lightweight and clear. It only has 3 KB and it is a nonminified version (a minified CSS or JS file is a version with comments, unnecessary spaces, and line breaks removed to reduce bandwidth). To create a sample RWD page, I will use both Bootstrap and Gridpak.

Twitter's Bootstrap, besides grids and reset styles, features a rich JavaScript component library. For this project, I need a responsive toolbar.

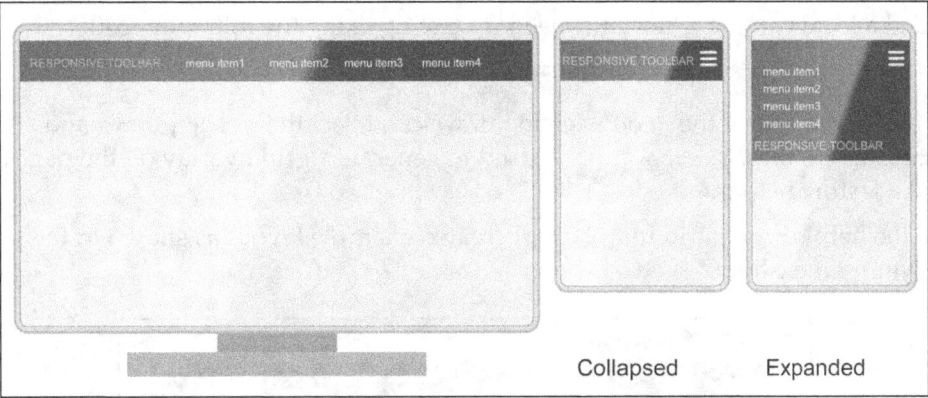

Responsive toolbar

The Bootstrap version without the grid system we created in the beginning of this chapter is the version we need now. The compile script is improved in this version and thanks to this, we had easily compiled a 27 KB version of `boostrap.css`.

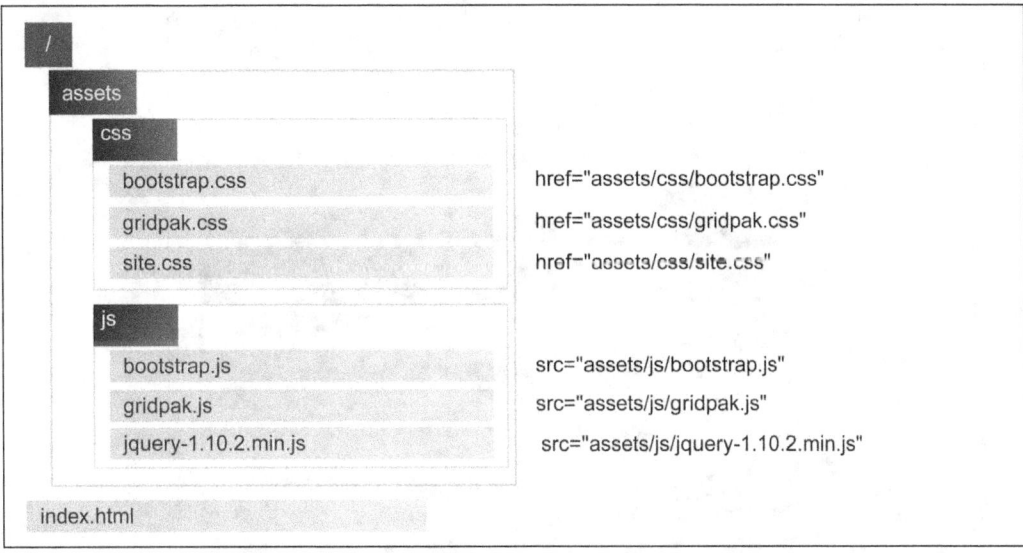

New website directory structure

As a base for the HTML template, we can use the Gridpak sample file. The following code helps us link the updated CSS files in the header. `site.css` is an empty stylesheet for website-specific CSS.

```
<link rel="stylesheet" media="all" type="text/css"
  href="assets/css/gridpak.css" />
<link rel="stylesheet" href="assets/css/bootstrap.css">
<link rel="stylesheet" href="assets/css/site.css">
```

I added a local copy of jQuery to speed up testing using the following code:

```
<script src="assets/js/jquery-1.10.2.min.js"></script>
```

Just before the end of the `<body>` element, we can inject the `gridpack.js` and `bootstrap js` files. `Gridpack.js` is used to generate a grid overlay on the page and is just a testing helper.

With the help of `.png` grid templates, I created a simple layout as shown in the following screenshot:

Fluid design we will code in this chapter

Implementing responsive design

To start the implementation process, I exported image files in their largest size (maximum assumed page width will be 2500px) and started to create the document structure, shown as follows:

```
<div class="page">
<!-- here we need navigation -->
  <div class="row">
    <div class="front_main_photo_wrapper col"></div>
  </div>
  <div class="row">
    <div class="photo_block4 item1 col">
      <img src="assets/img/img_front1_big.jpg"></div>
    <div class="photo_block4 item2 col">
      <img src="assets/img/img_front2_big.jpg"></div>
    <div class="photo_block4 item3 col">
      <img src="assets/img/img_front3_big.jpg"></div>
    <div class="photo_block4 item4 col">
      <img src="assets/img/img_front4_big.jpg"></div>
  </div>
  <div class="row">
    <div class="footer col"></div>
  </div>
</div>
```

Note that images inside these blocks became fluid without any action from our side. This happens because of H5BP CSS defaults, shown as follows:

```
img {
  max-width: 100%;
[...]
}
```

Classes `.row` and `.col` are Gridpak classes that set columns, margins, and padding according to the settings we created on `www.gridpak.com`. The class `.page` is the main content wrapper that can be used to define margins around content if we need them. An alternative way to define such margins may be by setting up padding on body elements. Bootstrap uses the following way for screens below 767px:

```
@media (max-width: 767px) {
  body {
    padding-right: 20px;
    padding-left: 20px;
  }
```

I'd like to set the left and right margins at five percent. Setting up padding on the body is the simplest way but it's not really a reliable or flexible way for this purpose (explaining this in detail is beyond the scope of this book). Instead I would try to control the content width with the following statement:

```
.page,bodydiv#gridpak{
  width:90%;
  margin:0px auto;
  padding:0 5% 0 5%;
}
```

Of course, to make the preceding code work as expected, it is necessary to comment out or override the Bootstrap `<body>` padding.

Classes `.photo_block4`, `.footer`, and `.front_main_photo_wrapper` are custom semantic names, and we have to define them within the respective media queries. This means that for each of the defined media query steps, we should decide how many columns wide the particular page block element should be. In our example, the class `photo_block4` will take the following size:

- 3 columns in resolution 800px to infinity
- 2 columns in resolution 320px to 800px
- 2 columns in resolution 320px and lower

Its translation to code is shown as follows:

```
inside: (min-width: 0px) and (max-width: 319px)
.photo_block4{width:48.5%;} /*same as .span_2 */
inside: @media screen and (min-width: 320px) and
  (max-width: 799px)
.photo_block4{width:23.5%;} /*same as .span_2 */
inside: @media screen and (min-width: 800px)
.photo_block4{width:24.25%;} /*same as .span_3 */
```

It works fine when the width is greater than 800px, where we have images in a row. There is however a problem when our four images are broken down into two or more rows. Gridpak uses the following CSS instruction to remove the left margin from the column class `.col`:

```
.row .col:first-child {margin-left:0;}
```

We have to take care of this ourselves in each media query where we see the problem, shown as follows:

```
@media screen and (min-width: 320px) and
  (max-width: 799px) {
  .row .col:first-child, .photo_block4.item3.col{
    margin-left:0;
  }
```

On this screen size, we start a new row from item three. For `max-width: 319px`, we can just merge `.photo_block4` definition with `.span_2`, as shown in the following code:

```
.span_2, .photo_block4 {
  margin-left:0;
  width:100%;
}
```

Now our blocks flow nicely across all resolutions. It's time to add some content using the following code:

```
<div class="main_photo">
  <img src="assets/img/photo_big.jpg">
</div>
```

The preceding HTML code is for the main photo. Please note that there is no `.col` class on the main photo div. In the original design, this photo extends to the full width of a container, `<div class="page">`. To avoid column padding, I just don't use the .col class. Actually, using Gridpak CSS for column padding is not very helpful in my design. But that is a good starting point and a reference when creating and coding design. At the end of the day, the code needs a cleanup, so I treat it as a part of the iterative process of building the page code. Most of the code in the bootstrap `reduced.css` can and should be removed before turning this example into a production code. Nonetheless, as we will use the `Carousel` component from this package, I leave it as is.

The following is the code for one of the blocks with a small photo:

```
<div class="photo_block4 item1 col">
  <img src="assets/img/img_front1_big.jpg">
    <h3>Rustical interiors</h3>
    <p>Loremipsum dolor sitamet, [...]. </p>
</div>
```

I don't describe CSS formatting for this block as it'd make this chapter unnecessarily long and complex. An issue related to CSS frameworks which is worth mentioning is the column padding problem. I needed the images above block headers to take full width using the `.col` class here, but this was an issue. To solve it, I override its default padding (coming from Grider stylesheet) in `site.css` by forcing all instances of `photo_block4 div` to have `padding:0px`. It is easier to add your own padding or margins to other elements of this block rather than trying to mess with negative margins. I just added the following code:

```css
.photo_block4 p{
  padding:0px 5%;
}
.photo_block4 h3{
  padding:0px 3%;
}
```

Our page needs a top responsive navigation bar, which is obtained using the following code:

```html
<div class="navbar navbar-inverse navbar-fixed-top">
  <div class="navbar-inner">
    <div class="page">
      <button type="button" class="btn btn-navbar"
        data-toggle="collapse" data-target=".nav-collapse">
        <span class="icon-bar"></span>
        <span class="icon-bar"></span>
        <span class="icon-bar"></span>
      </button>
      <a class="brand" href="#">Chatazapiecek</a>
      <div class="nav-collapse collapse">
        <ul class="nav">
          <li class="active"><a href="#">Home</a></li>
          <li><a href="#about">About</a></li>
          <li><a href="#contact">Contact</a></li>
        </ul>
      </div>
    </div>
  </div>
</div>
```

The preceding code is based on a sample from `http://twitter.github.com/bootstrap/examples/starter-template.html`. The Class `.navbar-fixed-top` causes the navigation bar to stay attached to the top of the window on wide screens. `<div class="page">` is the wrapper that constrains the navigation bar width to the same width as that of the page contents. The contents of `<div class="nav-collapse collapse">` are collapsed on small screens while `<button type="button" class="btn btn-navbar" data-toggle="collapse" data-target=".nav-collapse">` is shown to allow expanding this section.

An issue related to the navigation bar formatting is that fixed positioning on wide screens results in hiding a part of the page below it. To compensate for this effect, we can simply add the following code:

```
@media screen and (min-width: 979px){
  body{
    padding-top:70px;
  }
}
```

In this way we added the body element's top padding within the same media query as the navigation bar `position` changes to `fixed`.

For the final touch, I slightly adjusted the header font size to improve the page look in some resolutions using the following code:

```
@media screen and (max-width: 1200px) {
  .photo_block4 h3{
    font-size:18px;
    line-height:22px;
    padding-bottom:8px;
    padding-top:8px;
  }
}
```

To see the final document, please refer to the current chapter's resources directory. The page has a grid overlay on top. To hide it, just press G on the keyboard.

Summary

In this chapter, we created a sample HTML document that adjusts its layout to the screen size. We used Twitter's Bootstrap framework for its reset styles, default formatting, and responsive components library (here we employed just a responsive toolbar), and integrated it with a responsive grid created with the Gridpak tool. We still have some unsolved problems here, the most important of them being images. They scale nicely in all resolutions; however, when providing for a 320px screen size, images that look nice in resolutions above 2000px are a waste of bandwidth, device memory, and processing power. To optimize this, we will take a look at our Server Side options such as device detection libraries.

3

Server Side Setup – Device Detection Libraries

In this chapter we will discuss device detection libraries—tools that may help you to improve user experience on various devices.

In the previous chapter we created a responsive web document that adapts to screen resolution, but we didn't solve at least two issues, listed as follows:

- We use the same images for very large and very small screens; this means that, for a device that has a screen 320 px wide, we will download the 2500 px wide version anyway

- Our JavaScript and CSS elements are quite large, modern, and demanding in terms of processing power, browser capability, and memory, which though fine for most modern bleeding edge devices are still bad for older and cheaper phones.

To deal with this, we are going to use one of the old ways—a device detection library.

The history of the mobile web goes back over 10 years. The very first phones capable of browsing the Web used WAP with XHTML Mobile Profile as the document markup language instead of "normal" HTML over HTTP. Those days, making a website for mobile devices without Server Side mobile detection was simply impossible. Hence, Server Side device detection toolkits became indispensable for mobile web developers. Those libraries rely on parsing user agent strings; they map this information to device and browser capabilities and group them into groups with similar levels of support for content to be served. The two most well-known device databases are DeviceAtlas (available at www.deviceatlas.com) and WURFL.

The traditional way to serve content to mobile devices is based on the following elements:

- Mobile websites, usually on subdomains such as m.example.com
- Integrating a device detection library to look up device capabilities and assign them to groups (device classes) based on XHTML-MP, HTML5, image support, and so on
- Templates optimized for each device class
- Adapting content to ensure it is appropriate for a particular device class (resizing images and other media)

Both WURFL and DeviceAtlas are commercial solutions. A short comparison is shown in the following table:

Details	WURFL	DeviceAtlas
Free version available?	Yes	No (14-day trial available)
Free version limitations	• The cloud version has only 2 capabilities • 5.000 detections	Not Available
AGPL version available?	Yes, standalone version for PHP, .NET, and Java	No
Cloud version license plan pricing	0-500 USD/month	40-400 USD/month
OnSite version pricing	1,500-20,000 USD /month	Unknown

WURFL was, until Version 2.2, released under an open source/public domain license. As of August 30, 2011, it has dual license and updates are less frequent (the public version of the repository is updated once every 2-3 months). WURFL consists of two components, the resource file and APIs to access it. Dual license applies to standard APIs. The resource file is copyrighted by ScientiaMobile and commercial usage is strictly forbidden. The license also forbids any modification or use with non-standard AGPL-licensed APIs.

Translating this to plain English, it means that you can hardly use the standalone WURFL AGPL version for anything more than testing. If you decided to publish your work online, and if you think that your use is strictly non-commercial, you'd be required to publish your whole website code.

This change in licensing was the reason why WURFL support was dropped in the Zend Framework. Nonetheless, we can download and test this solution for ourselves.

The AGPL licensed "OnSite" version of the WURFL library

To download the WURFL file along with PHP APIs, go to `http://sourceforge.net/projects/wurfl/files/WURFL%20PHP/` and unpack the downloaded file (in my case it was `wurfl-php-1.4.4.0.zip`). You should see a directory structure as follows:

- docs\
- examples\
- tests\
- tools\
- WURFL\

Now we will integrate this with the web page created in *Chapter 2, Sample RWD Setup for Client-Side Development*. For the purpose of this example, I use the default setup for WampServer (available at `http://www.wampserver.com`). WampServer is a Windows web development environment based on the Apache server, MySQL database, and PHP. The web root is `C:\wamp\www\`. I created the `h5bpdemo` directory there, which will be our website's root directory. Our setup looks like the following:

- `c:\wamp\www`: The server document root
- `c:\wamp\www\h5bpdemo\`: The website base directory (website document root)
- `http://127.0.0.1/h5bpdemo/`: The HTTP website base directory
- `http://h5bp.test/`: The local domain `http://h5bp.test/` is achieved by adding this line of code to `C:\Windows\System32\drivers\etc\hosts`:

  ```
  127.0.0.1 h5bp.test
  ```

The following code is used to create the Vhost in `c:\wamp\bin\apache\apache2.2.22\conf\extra\httpd-vhosts.conf`:

```
<VirtualHost *:80>
    ServerAdmin webmaster@dummy-host.example.com
    DocumentRoot "c:/wamp/www/h5bpdemo/"
    ServerName h5bp.test
</VirtualHost>
```

Also the following needs to be uncommented in `c:\wamp\bin\apache\apache2.2.22\conf\extra\httpd-vhosts.conf`:

```
#Include conf/extra/httpd-vhosts.conf
```

Before I delve into details, I should define the purpose of the application I'm about to create. It should help me solve issues some visitors might have when they visit my website. So first I have to learn something about the devices my customers are using. I live in Europe and I assume my customers come from Europe too. To get some up-to-date statistics about the mobile browsers they use, I go to `http://gs.statcounter.com` and look for last month's mobile browser statistics. In these statistics, iPhone, Android, and Opera lead in March 2013. In some countries, around or over 10 percent usage is via Blackberry (UK 15 percent) and Nokia (Albania 10 percent). This is good news because all these are HTML-enabled browsers and we won't need any WML templates. Some of the code in the RWD sample uses JavaScript to manipulate document structure. I also used modern CSS to format the document. It may not work on some older devices. I decided to group my devices into the following three categories:

- **Basic**: XHTML with basic CSS
- **Medium**: XHTML with decent CSS and image support
- **Advanced**: HTML5 with CSS Level 3 and good JavaScript support (AJAX-manipulating DOM structure)

At the moment, I'm not going to deal with image resizing. There is a separate chapter devoted to that. Here I will just use the preceding three templates to adjust HTML and CSS markup and attach JavaScript only for devices that can really understand it. I'm going to test several solutions, and my application structure should allow for easy swapping from one library to another.

After copying files from the previous chapter, I added directories for the Server Side code, so it now is shown as follows:

- `/app/`: My Server Side application directory
- `/app/bootstrap.php`: The loader for the Server Side application
- `/app/config.php`: The general configuration file for this application
- `/app/libs/`: For Server Side libraries
- `/app/libs/WURFL/`: APIs from `wurfl-php-1.4.4.0.zip`
- `/app/templates/`: For partial templates
- `/app/wurfl_onsite/`: The directory for my app module based on standalone WURFL AGPL
- `/app/wurfl_onsite/app.php`: My class wrapper for WURFL API
- `/app/wurfl_onsite/config.php`: The configuration file for this module based on `examples\demo\inc\wurfl_config_standard.php`, which is in the official API package

- `/app/wurfl_onsite/resources/`: The location for the WURFL file with device descriptions
- `/app/wurfl_onsite/resources/storage/`: Internal WURFL PHP API storage
- `/app/wurfl_test.php`: Test page using the WURFL PHP API
- `/assets/`: here we have all JavaScript, CSS, and images created in the previous chapter

The file `wurfl_test.php` will be the test page for our website WURFL library. Boostrap will help us to inject into this page the ability to detect the device class. To be able to change the device detection library without changing the Bootstrap code (and to be able to test at the same time), I created a very simple loader function inside `bootstrap.php` shown as:

```
function getDDLobject($library) {
  if ($library=='wurfl_onsite') //later I can add other
  {
    require_once APPLICATION_DIR.'wurfl_onsite/app.php';
    $DDLobject=new Mod_Wurfl_Onsite();
    return $DDLobject;
  }
}
```

Now in `/wurfl_on_site.php`, I can get `$DDLobject` (the device detection library object) by writing the following code:

```
include "app/bootstrap.php";
$DDLobject = getDDLobject('wurfl_onsite');
```

This object is an instance of a custom class that is a wrapper for provider APIs. It allows us to build our own classifications based on defined requirements. But to use it we need to first create our `Mod_Wurfl_Onsite` class. This will reside in `APPLICATION_DIR`. The constant `'wurfl_onsite/app.php'`. The `APPLICATION_DIR` directory is defined in the application config file, `/app/conf.php`. The class uses a few internal member variables, shown in the following code:

```
protected $config;
protected $wurfl_config;
protected $wurfl_manager;
protected $wurfl_device;
```

$config is a convenience configuration data container that we pass to $this->config in the constructor shown in the following code:

```
function __construct() {
  include dirname(__FILE__)."/conf.php";
  $this->config=&$config;
  $this->createWurflObject();
}
```

In the constructor we load the configuration data from APPLICATION_DIR.'wurfl_onsite/conf.php using the following code:

```
$config['MOD_DIR'] = APPLICATION_DIR.'wurfl_onsite/';
$config['MOD_NAME'] = 'wurfl_onsite/';
$config['WURFL_API_DIR'] = LIBRARIES_DIR.'WURFL/';
$config['WURFL_RESOURCES_DIR'] =
  $config['MOD_DIR'].'resources/';
$config['WURFL_RESOURCE_FILE'] =
  $config['WURFL_RESOURCES_DIR'].'wurfl.zip';
$config['WURFL_STORAGE_DIR'] =
  $config['WURFL_RESOURCES_DIR'].'storage/';
$config['WURFL_CACHE_DIR'] =
  $config['WURFL_STORAGE_DIR'].'cache/';
$config['WURFL_PERSISTENCE_DIR'] =
  $config['WURFL_STORAGE_DIR'].'persistence/';
```

Basically these are the directories that WURFL uses. The OnSite version of WURFL parses the XML device description file contained in wurfl.zip to create a cache during the first launch. To use this data in the function createWurflObject(), we load the WURFL API (require_once ($this->config['WURFL_API_DIR'].'Application.php ');), create WURFL_Configuration_InMemoryConfig, and assign to it the configuration data as shown in the following code:

```
function createWurflObject() {
  require_once ($this->config['WURFL_API_DIR'].
    'Application.php '); //load WURFL API
  $this->wurfl_config = new
    WURFL_Configuration_InMemoryConfig();
  $this->wurfl_config->wurflFile($this->config[
    'WURFL_RESOURCE_FILE']);
  $this->wurfl_config->persistence('file',
    array('dir' => $this->config['WURFL_PERSISTENCE_DIR']));
  $this->wurfl_config->cache('file',
    array('dir' => $this->config['WURFL_CACHE_DIR'],
  'expiration' => 36000));
  $this->wurfl_config->matchMode('performance');
  // Set the match mode for the API ('performance'
    or 'accuracy')
  $this->wurfl_config->allowReload(true);
```

With all the necessary options assigned, we just pass this object to the WURFL_ WURFLManagerFactory constructor as shown in the following code:

```
$wurflManagerFactory =
  new WURFL_WURFLManagerFactory($this->wurfl_config);
```

With the WURFL_WURFLManagerFactory instance, we can create the wurfl_manager instance and store it in our class variable as follows:

```
$this->wurfl_manager = $wurflManagerFactory->create();
}
```

We are now almost ready to read device capabilities. I created a method for this, named getDeviceClass(), as shown in the following code. It returns one of the four strings describing the device, that is, the name of one of our device groupings (classes) plus unsupported in case we are dealing with some really old device and can't use HTML at all (as we had originally decided to create only HTML versions).

```
function getDeviceClass() {
  $this->wurfl_device =
    $this->wurfl_manager->getDeviceForHttpRequest($_SERVER);
  $xhtml_level = $this->wurfl_device-
    >getCapability('xhtml_support_level');
  if ($xhtml_level<0) {
    return 'unsupported';
  }
  if ($xhtml_level<3) {
    return 'basic';
  }
}
```

To start with, I pass the $_ SERVER PHP environment variable to the $this- >wurfl_manager-> getDeviceForHttpRequest method. It returns to us the wurfl_device instance we can query for device capabilities. To do this we need to learn what capabilities we can ask for. There is a list of those available at http:// wurfl.sourceforge.net/help_doc.php. The capability xhtml_support_level is the easiest and most important from our point of view. Each of the capabilities may have a different set of possible values. xhtml_support_level has one of the six levels represented as an integer in the range [-1,4]. The description of the levels is as follows:

- **Level -1**: This means that there is no XHTML support of any kind.
- **Level 0**: This gives us basic XHTML support with no or very unreliable CSS support.
- **Level 1**: This has XHTML with some CSS support. Hyperlinks may not be colorable by CSS. The minimum screen width is 120 pixels.

- **Level 2**: This is generally the same as level 1.
- **Level 3**: It has excellent CSS support.
- **Level 4**: It consists of Level 3 plus Ajax support.

I assigned the preceding levels to our groupings as shown in the following table:

Group name	Level	Comments
Unsupported	-1	
Basic	0, 1, and 2	The template for the basic group can only contain very basic HTML.
Medium	3 and 4	It consists of level 3 and level 4 elements without confirmed and good JavaScript capabilities. For testing this I use two other capabilities, ajax_manipulate_dom and ajax_support_events. Originally I wanted to also use css_rounded_corners and css_gradient but rounded corners turned out to be unreliable and css_gradient didn't work at all in the public version of the PHP API. The template for the medium group can be the same as for the advanced group but with removed jQuery and without JavaScript-related CSS.
Advanced	4	It consists of level 4 elements with ajax_manipulate_dom and ajax_support_events capabilities. The template for the advanced group remains unchanged.

According to the preceding table, testing for advanced and medium groups is slightly more complex, as shown in the following code:

```
if ($xhtml_level>=3) {
  $css_ajax_dom_support =
    $this->wurfl_device->getCapability(
    'ajax_manipulate_dom');
  $css_ajax_events_support =
    $this->wurfl_device->getCapability(
    'ajax_support_events');
  if(($xhtml_level==4)
    &&$css_ajax_events_support
    &&$css_ajax_dom_support) {
    return 'advanced';
  } else {
    return 'medium';
  }
}
```

The WURFL Cloud version

There is a limited free offering from ScientaMobile that can be used commercially by microbusinesses. To get access to it, it is necessary to register at https://www.scientiamobile.com/cloud/signup/free. After confirming the e-mail address, log in to http://www.scientiamobile.com, go to your account page, and after clicking on your account name, you can find your API key and download the client code. We can use two capabilities with the free account and we need to add them to our account.

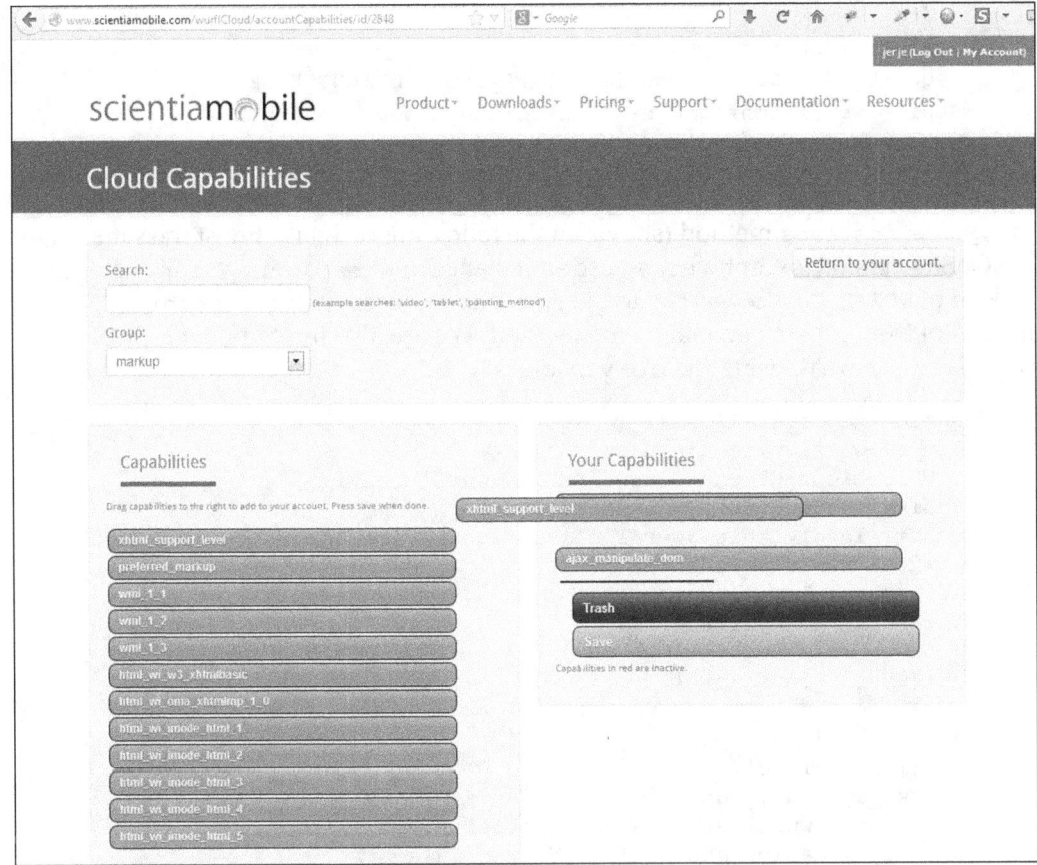

The Scientia mobile capabilities screen

Let's follow the **Cloud Capabilities** link on the left. On the **Capabilities** page, from the drop-down menu, select **markup** to drag **xhtml_support_level** to the **Your Capabilities** area. Then, similarly select **Ajax** in the drop-down menu and drag the capability **ajax_manipulate_dom** to the **Your Capabilities** area.

We assign the API key (copied from **Account Settings | API keys**) to a private member variable of our class, which is shown as follows:

```
class Mod_Wurfl_Cloud {
  private static $api_key ='
    '644333:XXXXXnUqrX6YsZfViS2cert3o0XXXXX';//instead of
    this API key please use your own
```

Our `createWurflObject` method is much shorter now, as seen in the following code. There is no device factory class in the cloud API, and we only create the `config` object relying on defaults.

```
function createWurflObject() {
  require_once $this->config['WURFL_CLOUD_CLIENT_FILE'];
  $this->wurfl_config = new WurflCloud_Client_Config();
  $this->wurfl_config->api_key = self::$api_key;
}
```

The `getDeviceClass` method (shown in the following code) is almost the same as in the OnSite version, except we now use an instance of `WurflCloud_Client_Client` instead of `WURFL_CustomDevice` to query device features with `getCapability` instead of the `getDeviceCapability` method. We are also limited now to two capabilities, as we're using the free version.

```
function getDeviceClass() {
  $this->wurfl_client = new
    WurflCloud_Client_Client($this->wurfl_config);
  $this->wurfl_client->detectDevice();
  $xhtml_level=$this->wurfl_client->getDeviceCapability('
    xhtml_support_level');
  if ($xhtml_level<0) {
    return 'unsuported';
  }
  if ($xhtml_level<3) {
    return 'basic';
  }
  if ($xhtml_level>=3) {
    $css_ajax_dom_support =
      $this->wurfl_device->getCapability(
      'ajax_manipulate_dom'); // true/false
    if (($xhtml_level==4)&&$css_ajax_dom_support) {
      return 'advanced';
    } else {
      return 'medium';
    }
  }
}
```

YABFDL – Detector

Detector or "yet another browser and feature- detection library" by Dave Olsen, available at `https://github.com/dmolsen/Detector`, represents quite a different approach to the same problem. Instead of relying on centrally updated, database-binding UA strings to device capabilities, it uses JavaScript feature detection, stores collected information in the session variable, and saves it to the local cache. The most important features include:

- Combining Server Side and Client Side browser-feature detection
- A free, open, and very permissive license
- Automatically updates the device list upon unknown device visit
- The Detector relies on the JavaScript `modernizr.js`

Detector is in the Beta version and is not updated very often but is worth attention, especially when your target devices are JavaScript capable. The 5477 **User Agent (UA)** profiles registered by Detector until today seem modest in comparison to the 1,200,000 UA profiles in the 51degrees database (`http://51degrees.mobi`; 51degrees is a solution similar to DeviceAtlas or WURFL), but Detector's autoupdate feature allows support to all browsers that are able to parse the `modernizr.js` script.

Detector's process of detecting browser features works in the following three steps:

- If there is an open session for this visitor, the feature list from the session variable is used
- If there is no valid session, the UA string is checked against a list of UAs that have already visited the website, and if a match is found, a related feature list is used
- If there is no match, Modernizr tests are being sent to the browser; the result is saved in a cookie, the page is reloaded, and the data is saved on the server

Detector is very easy to set up and integrate. After downloading Detector from `https://github.com/dmolsen/Detector` and extracting the ZIP file, we have to copy the contents of the `Detector0XX/lib/Detector/` directory to our library's directory, `app/libs/Detector`. Following the pattern from the last example, we will also create the `app/detector` directory for `conf.php` and `app.php`. In this case `conf.php` needs to just hold the library directory, as shown in the following code:

```
$config['DETECTOR_API_DIR'] = LIBRARIES_DIR.'detector/';
```

Creating `detector` in the `Mod_Detector` class inside `app.php` is simple too, as shown in the following code:

```
function createDetector() {
  require_once ($this->config['DETECTOR_API_DIR'].
    'Detector.php');
  $this->detector_ua = $ua;
}
```

With `$this->detector_ua`, we can read device properties using the following code:

```
if($this->detector_ua->fontface) {
  echo '@font-face allowed';
}
```

CSS3 Features	Your Browser	Detector Profile
backgroundsize:	TRUE	TRUE
bgrepeatround:	FALSE	FALSE
bgrepeatspace:	FALSE	FALSE
bgsizecover:	FALSE	FALSE
borderimage:	TRUE	TRUE
borderradius:	TRUE	TRUE
boxshadow:	TRUE	TRUE
boxsizing:	TRUE	TRUE
cssanimations:	TRUE	TRUE
csscolumns:	TRUE	TRUE
cssgradients:	TRUE	TRUE
cssreflections:	FALSE	FALSE
cssremunit:	TRUE	TRUE
cssresize:	TRUE	TRUE
cssscrollbar:	FALSE	FALSE
csstransforms:	TRUE	TRUE
csstransforms3d:	TRUE	TRUE
csstransitions:	TRUE	TRUE
cubicbezierrange:	TRUE	TRUE
flexbox:	FALSE	FALSE

Detection and the Evolution of Responsive Web Design
* Why I Created Detector
* @dmolsen on Twitter

Credits

Detector is based on Modernizr, modernizr-server, and the browser-detection library ua-parser-php. It also benefits from a healthy dose of inspiration from Yiibu's Profile.

Share This

Tweet 401
Like 88
+1 35

Archive

The following 5477 user agent profiles are already in the system (readable list):

* ...
* AppleWebKit/530.17 (KHTML, l...
* BlackBerry8520/5.0.0.1036 Pr...
* BlackBerry8520/5.0.0.681 Pro...
* BlackBerry8520/5.0.0.681 Pro...
* BlackBerry8520/5.0.0.681 Pro...
* BlackBerry9000/5.0.0.93 Prof...
* BlackBerry9360/7.0.0.590 Pro...
* BlackBerry9650/4.4.0.185 Pro...
* BlackBerry9700/5.0.0.593 Pro...
* BlackBerry9700/5.0.0.656 Pro...
* BlackBerry9800/6.0.0.337 Pro...
* Chimera/2.0alpha
* Fauxzilla 1.0
* FeedFetcher-Google; (http:/...
* Gigabot/3.0 (http://www.giga...
* HTC Desire HD Android 2.2.1...
* IUC(U;iOS 5.1.1;Zh-cn;320*48...
* IUC(U;iOS 6.1;Zh-cn;320*480;...
* JUC (Linux; U; 2.3.5; zh-cn...

Detector's CSS3 detected features list

All device capability tests in Detector return only `true` or `false`. There is nothing resembling the `xhtml_support_level` WURFL capability. In fact, we should not expect any information about devices with no or very basic XHTML support from this library. Checking the strings of UA's registered on `http://detector.dmolsen.com/` against the WURFL `xhtml_support_level` feature shows that all of them have a value of 3.

At the same time, their level of support for CSS and HTML5 properties varies a lot and we can check it very precisely to learn, for example, whether a particular browser supports @font-face, text-shadow, CSS gradients, and so on.

Before using this library we need to take into account the following factors:

- Whether it is in Beta version and requires some real testing before it can be used in the production code
- Whether it is only for relatively modern phones, not those older than three years (it works only with browsers with JavaScript and cookies support)

Whether this library can be useful for us depends on the preceding factors.

The good news is that now, in March 2013, it should work for more than 90 percent of global mobile browsers, as can be seen at the following link:

`http://gs.statcounter.com/#mobile_browser-ww-monthly-201202-201303`

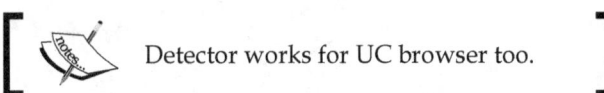 Detector works for UC browser too.

Summary

Using custom wrapper classes, we integrated three device detection libraries into a simple but consistent environment. Now we are ready to fine-tune our mobile groups and start building our RESS application. In the next chapter we will create four simple RESS solutions, each based on another library or method to detect User Agent features.

4
Sample RESS Page

In this chapter we focus on the information flow in an RESS application. We take a closer look at the possible strategies in building an RESS application and we create four sample scenarios based on WURFL, Detector, or just on simple JavaScript.

There is no strict definition of what an RESS system is, except that it uses a mixture of Server Side and Client Side device optimization. The idea is to build a pragmatic approach that allows better adjustment of RWD page components to some device classes.

We need to define the practical purposes of our RESS system, which are as follows:

1. Adjusting a document to device capabilities (HTML markup, CSS level, and JavaScript code). This particularly means:

    °   Creating simplistic markup for older devices, for those with very limited screen size, and for those with a slow processor, to ensure that the page is displayed on all devices that support any kind of HTML markup

    °   Optimization of markup for devices that support modern constructs

    °   Using jQuery components when it is possible

2. Adjusting media (images in our case) to device screen width.

3. Allowing manual selection of the page version (lower, if the customer wishes to reduce bandwidth to minimum possible value or higher, if the customer wishes to try the enhanced version).

To fulfill the preceding tasks we can use various solutions. In this chapter we will discuss the following four approaches:

- WURFL plus screen size detection
- Dave Olsen's Detector
- The simplest possible approach, based only on JavaScript screen size detection and fallback to a simplistic page if this fails
- Dave Olsen's Detector plus WURFL

WURFL plus screen size detection

We use the same framework setup for our test RESS applications as we did in the previous chapter with device detection libraries. You can find it in the directory ress_cookie_wurfl with the class Ress_Cookie_Wurfl in app.php. I added a generalized apploader to bootstrap.php. The Apploader (application loader) in this case is just a function in bootstrap.php that takes the module name as an argument and returns a module class instance. We can now get the Ress_Cookie_Wurfl class instance from my test page ress_cookie_wurfl.php with the following line of code:

```
$RESS_app1 = loadApp('ress_cookie_wurfl');
```

We start processing the request by checking if a cookie exists and if it does, we save this value to a class variable, as in the following code:

```
if (array_key_exists('screen_width', $_COOKIE)) {
  $cookie_screen_width = $_COOKIE['screen_width'];
  $this->screen_width = $cookie_screen_width;
  $this->cookie_exists = true;
}
```

If for some reason we don't have a cookie, we use the following code:

```
else {
  $this->screen_width=$this->getWurflWidth();
}
```

The getWurflWidth() function loads our custom Mod_Wurfl_Onsite class and checks the default screen width, as in the following code:

```
function getWurflWidth() {
  $this->wurfl_object = getDDLobject('wurfl_onsite');
  return $this->wurfl_object-
    >getDeviceCapability('resolution_width');
}
```

As bootstrap.php should already be loaded, we can use the getDDLobject() global function to load our Wurfl_Onsite library wrapper and read the default screen width based on the UA string.

To save the screen size in a cookie, it is enough to put a few lines of JavaScript like this:

```
<script type="text/javascript">
  var RESS_a = {};
  RESS_a.width = window.innerWidth;
  RESS_a.setCookie=function(name,value,days){
    var Cdate=new Date();
    Cdate.setDate(Cdate.getDate() + days);
    var c_value=value + ((days==null) ? "" : ";
      expires ="+Cdate.toUTCString());
    document.cookie=name + "=" + c_value;
  }
  RESS_a.setCookie("screen_width",RESS_a.width,30)
</script>
```

With this code we create the RESS_a object, which allows us to separate our setCookie function from other JavaScript we might wish to attach to the page later.

The following figure shows the information flow in this scenario. We are only interested in obtaining the actual screen width. Using WURFL just for this purpose seems both unreliable and overshot. In most cases, we could probably just rely on JavaScript or use some safe fallback in case it doesn't work. The problem is that we'd have to force reload a page (in a similar way that the Detector does in the following sample) risking getting into a reload loop.

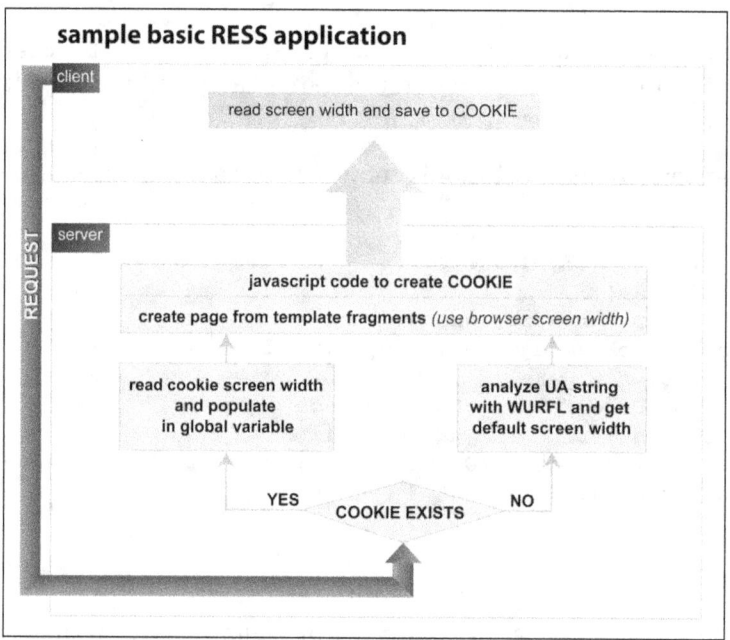

Dave Olsen's Detector

The Detector library is an attempt to make device detection libraries based on the analysis of UA strings obsolete. The problem with this is that it needs to send the test page to a browser that supports JavaScript and has it turned on. In order to speed up the page loading, it employs the following two mechanisms:

- Using the server cache of UA string footprints (which ironically makes it, in a way, a UA string analysis library)
- Storing client information in both a session variable and a cookie

The following figure illustrates information flow between the Detector and the browser. The HTTP request drawn on the left side represents the first and each consecutive "regular" request. The one drawn on the right side is sent from the test page and may occur as a second request when none of the conditions in the center of the figure is met. In other words when the user requests any page on the website, Detector tries to determine the following:

- If cookies and JavaScript are supported
- If this user visited this website before (browser data is then cached in a session variable)
- If the User Agent footprint and the relevant profile are cached in the system

If all these checks fail, Detector sends a test page instead of the regular one. The test page executes the reload and returns missing information in the next request. After the test request, the original (regular) page is sent to the browser.

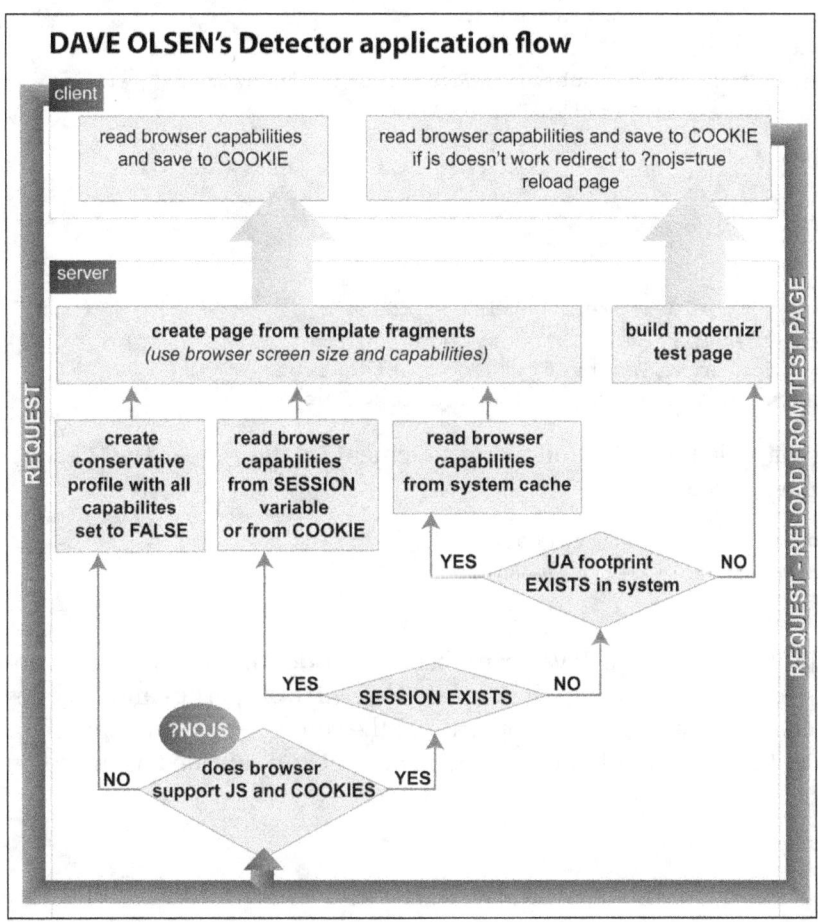

The first check (as shown in the preceding figure), **does browser support JS and COOKIES**, is based on checking for the `nojs = true` parameter using the following code:

```
(isset($_REQUEST["nojs"]) && ($_REQUEST["nojs"] == "true"))
  || (isset($_REQUEST["nocookies"]) &&
  ($_REQUEST["nocookies"] == "true"
```

This may come the test for JavaScript support in the form of the following code:

```
<noscript><meta http-equiv='refresh' content='0;
  url=".self::buildNoscriptLink()."'></noscript>
```

Or it may come from the JavaScript test for cookie support in the browser (in `/app/libs/Detector/lib/modernizr/cookieTest.js`), using the following code:

```
function getCookie() {
  var i,x,y,ARRcookies=document.cookie.split(";");
  for (i=0;i<ARRcookies.length;i++)
    {x=ARRcookies[i].substr(0,ARRcookies[i].indexOf("="));
    y=ARRcookies[i].substr(ARRcookies[i].indexOf("=")+1);
    x=x.replace(/^\s+|\s+$/g,"");
    if (x == "testCookie") {
      return y;
    }
  }
}
document.cookie = "testCookie=testData";
var cookieRedirect = (window.location.href.match(/\?/))
  ? window.location.href + "&nocookies=true" :
  window.location.href + "?nocookies=true";
```

The code is applied with the following statement (in the `/app/libs/Detector/Detector.php` library):

```
if (getCookie() != 'testData') {
=window.location = cookieRedirect;
}
```

But a majority chunk of the JavaScript (besides Modernizr itself) is a function _mer based on the Modernizr server. It iterates Modernizr properties and encodes those that are recognized as browser properties to the cookie. After decoding them on the server-side, they are stored in the `stdclass` object and returned as the `$ua` variable in `Detector.php`.

As with the other examples, I use the same module and directory structure that allows us to create a module class instance with the function loadApp($appName) from the file bootstrap.php.

To actually use the Detector library, I put the files downloaded from https://github.com/dmolsen/Detector to the app/libs/Detector directory. I then created the Ress_Detector class in the app/ress_detector/app.php file. This class is essentially nothing more than a simple wrapper for the Detector library that allows us to use some of its functions via an interface consistent with other examples. In the member function createDetector() called from the constructor, we include Detector.php and assign the $ua variable to the class property detector_ua, as in the following code:

```
function createDetector() {
    require_once ($this->config['DETECTOR_API_DIR'].
      'Detector.php');//load WURFL API
    $this->detector_ua=&$ua;
}
```

In this way we can easily pull Detector information of interest to us, anywhere inside the Ress_Detector class. Member functions of this class shown in the following code facilitate accessing browser properties via a consistent interface (by consistent interface, I mean here keeping the same signatures of the key methods in all the examples in this chapter. This allows easy swapping of detection modules without breaking the application).

```
function getDeviceClass() {
    return $this->detector_ua->family;
}
function getScreenWidth() {
    return $this->detector_ua->screenattributes->windowWidth;
}
function getDeviceCapability($name) {
    if(isset($this->detector_ua->$name))
    {
        return $this->detector_ua->$name;
    } else {
        return null;
    }
}
```

All the preceding code in this section may be contained inside the template as in the following code:

```php
<?php include "app/bootstrap.php";
$RESS_detector = loadApp('ress_detector');
?>
  <body>
    <p>device class: <?php echo $RESS_detector->
      getDeviceClass(); ?></p>
    <p>screen width: <?php echo $RESS_detector->
      getScreenWidth(); ?></p>
    <p>fontface: <?php $fontface = $RESS_detector->
      getDeviceCapability("fontface") ;
    echo $fontface?"supported":"not supported"; ?></p>
  </body>
```

Pure JavaScript screen size test

In this approach, we don't use any external libraries. We don't test for browser capabilities as in the first example; we are only concerned with the screen width. The purpose here is to create something simple and extendable at the same time. The PHP code for the two main classes have less than 100 lines, and a test page set to the browser for reload has less than 1.5 KB in a non-minified state with all the JavaScript included. You can use the code from this example as a starting point for building your own tests best suited to your situation, without worrying about third-party licenses or library updates. I tried to make it as simple and safe as possible. In case of any problems, the result of the check will change to the basic version and a 120 px screen width.

The following figure shows the program flow; you can see that the logic is very similar to that of the Detector. This simplified version doesn't store UA profiles in the local cache.

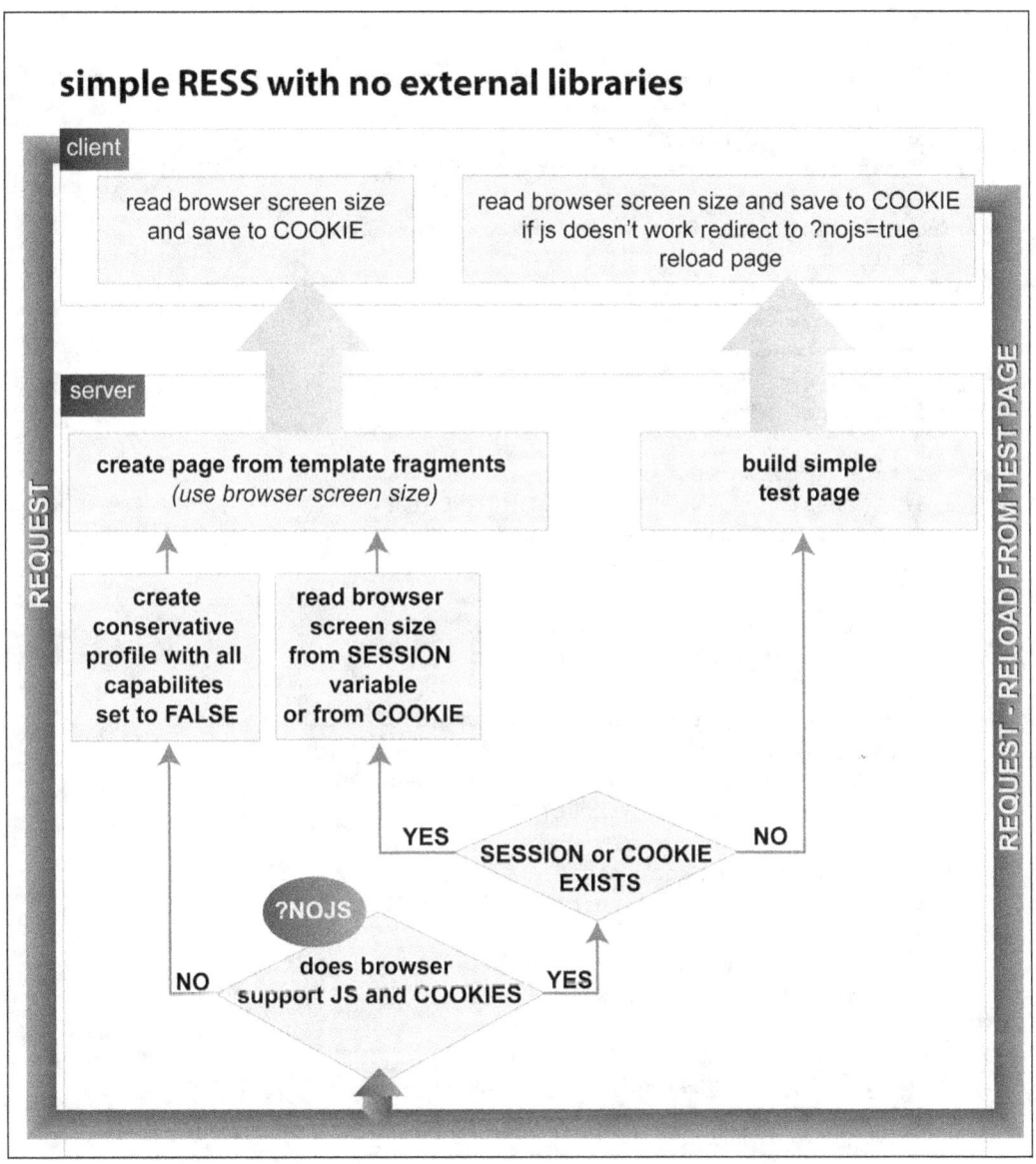

The application structure is built around the same framework as our other samples. Processing HTTP requests (checks for Cookies and so on) is moved to the constructor of a separate `Request` class, as in the following code:

```
class Request
{
//true when in $_GET exists any of parameters:
 testreload | nocookies | nojs
public $from_test_page;
// if has session containing screen_width var
public $has_session;
//(no cookies or no js - will not work for us)
  defaults to true
public $simplistic_browser = true;
//does it have our cookie
public $has_cookie;
// very low default
public $screen_width = 120;

  function __construct() {
    if (@session_start() && isset($_SESSION)
    && array_key_exists('screen_width',$_SESSION)
    && ($_SESSION['screen_width'] >0))
    {
      $this->screen_width = $_SESSION['screen_width'];
      $this->has_session = true;
    }
    if (array_key_exists('screen_width',$_COOKIE)) {
      $this->screen_width = $_COOKIE["screen_width"];
      $_SESSION['screen_width'] = $this->screen_width;
      $this->has_session = true;
    }
//it is request from test page
    if (array_key_exists('testreload',$_GET))
    {
      $this->from_test_page = true;
      $this->simplistic_browser = false;
    }
    elseif (array_key_exists('nocookies',$_GET) ||
      array_key_exists('nojs',$_GET)) {
      $this->from_test_page = true;
    } else {
      $this->from_test_page = false;
    }
  }
}
```

This code is pretty self-explanatory — we check for a session, then for a cookie, and then we verify if this was called from the test page and if the browser supports JavaScript and cookies. Writing JavaScript and HTML code inside class methods is ugly and hard to maintain; hence, I created the `assets` directory inside this module's directory. Inside it you can find the following files:

- `test_page.js`: JavaScript to be placed inside the header of our browser test page
- `testpage.php`: The HTML markup for our test page. Inside the HTML `header` section of this file we inject the contents of `test_page.js`
- `cookie.js`: The JavaScript code to be placed inside the HTML header of all pages on the website (to update the screen width with each request)

Code contained in the `test_page.js` file is supposed to save the screen width in a cookie, if that is possible, or redirect the page to the same address but with the `?nocookies=true` string appended to the URL (this way we send the `nocookies` variable of type string with value "true" as a URL parameter. In PHP we access it via the `_GET` array). Inside the `cookie_enabled` function shown in the following code, I used a simpler and more dependable method of detecting cookie support in the browser. First, checking whether the document cookie exists in the browser DOM and then if we can save anything there.

Please note that in the following code, the `RESS_pure_js.cookie_enabled = function()` construct is used instead of the plain `function bakeCookie()`. We do it this way to keep all our functions inside a separate namespace, ensuring that we will not get in conflict with some other JavaScript code that might (in the future) find a way of getting here.

```
var RESS_pure_js={};
RESS_pure_js.cookie_enabled = function()
{
  document.cookie = "testcookie";
  cookieEnabled = ("cookie" in document
    && (document.cookie.length > 0
    || (document.cookie =
    "test").indexOf(document.cookie, "test") > -1));
  return cookieEnabled;
}
```

The function `bakeCookie` is called in the last line of `test_page.js`.

Inside the RESS_pure_js.bakeCookie() function shown in the following code, we call cookie_enabled to check for browser cookie support. If the test fails, we reload the page but with the ?nocookies=true string appended to the URL. Actually, we append either the ?nocookies=true or the &nocookies=true string depending on whether the URL contains ? already or not. If the test passes, we save the screen width information inside the else section. If we'd like to save other information in the cookie too, we do it inside the same code block (the else section).

```
RESS_pure_js.bakeCookie = function(){
  if (!this.cookie_enabled())
  {
    var linkNoCookies=(window.location.href.match(/\?/))
      ? window.location.href + "&nocookies = true":
      window.location.href + "?nocookies=true";
    window.location = linkNoCookies;
  } else {
    this.width = window.innerWidth;
    this.setCookie("screen_width", this.width, 30);
  }
}
```

The setCookie function is the same as in the previous example.

The JavaScript code from the test_page.js file is injected inside the HTML header element of testpage.php. We still need to check for JavaScript support with Meta refresh, exactly the same way as in the second approach (that is, Dave Olsen's Detector).

When the browser supports both JavaScript and Cookies, we refresh the page with JavaScript. Appending the ?testreload=true string to the URL adds testreload to the GET variables. The value of testreload is a string "true". Using this parameter ensures that HTTP requests from the test page can easily be recognized on the server side and the reload loop can be avoided. The following snippet demonstrates the JavaScript reload code:

```
function delayed_reload() {
  var linkReload = (window.location.href.match(/\?/))
    ? window.location.href + "&testreload=true" :
    window.location.href + "?testreload=true";
  window.location = linkReload;
}
[...]
<body onLoad="setTimeout('delayed_reload()', 500)">
```

The JavaScript that checks for the screen width inside the file `cookie.js` — the one that is attached to regular pages — is slightly different than the one on the test page. We don't do any redirects here; we just notify our server-side application if the window size has changed or not, hence removing code checking for cookies support, URL rewriting, and redirecting. Instead, as seen in the following code, there is the added `onresize` event to update information in the cookie, in case the user has changed the width of the window. It's being done with some delay. Updating cookies each 0.5 seconds seems enough and reduces unnecessary processor load.

```
var RESS_pure_js={};
RESS_pure_js.bakeCookie = function(){
  this.width = window.innerWidth;
  this.setCookie("screen_width", this.width, 30);
}
// setCookie function
RESS_pure_js.setCookie=function(name,value,days) {
  var Cdate=new Date();
  Cdate.setDate(Cdate.getDate() + days);
  var c_value=value + ((days==null) ? "" : "; expires="+Cdate.
toUTCString());
  document.cookie=name + "=" + c_value;
}
RESS_pure_js.bakeCookie()
window.onresize = function(event) {
  setTimeout('RESS_pure_js.bakeCookie()', 500)
}
```

With such an in-depth understanding of the way we transmit information about the browser to the server and with the `Request` class instance created, all we need to do is ask for this information from our class `Ress_Pure_Js` (a module class that is instantiated in the "page file" via the calling function `loadApp($appName)` in `bootstrap.php`). The following methods of the `Ress_Pure_Js` class can provide us with the necessary information:

```
function getScreenWidth() {
  return $this->request->screen_width;
}
function getDeviceClass() {
  if ($this->request->simplistic_browser)
  {
    return 'basic';
  } else {
    return 'advanced';
  }
}
```

We should not forget to create and send the test page in case we didn't do it yet with this visitor using the following code:

```php
function __construct() {
  include dirname(__FILE__)."/conf.php";
  $this->config = &$config;
  $this->request = new Request();
  if (!$this->request->has_session &&
    !$this->request->from_test_page)
  {
    $this->build_test_page();
  }
}
private function build_test_page()
{
  $this->cookie_test_js = @file_get_contents ($this-
    >config['MOD_ASSETS_DIR']."test_page.js");
  $test_page_template =$this-
    >config['MOD_ASSETS_DIR']."testpage.php";
  include $test_page_template;
  exit;
}
```

In the `build_test_page` function we include `testpage.php` to execute it in the scope of this function and then with `exit;` we immediately send the output to the browser.

Utility functions

The `getNoJsUrl` function is a safe way to add a `nojs=true` parameter to the current URL, and it looks like this:

```php
function getNoJsUrl()
{
  $get_parameters = array('nojs'=>'true');
  $get_parameters = array_merge($get_parameters,$_GET);
  list($clean_url) = explode("?", $_SERVER["REQUEST_URI"]);
  return $clean_url."?".http_build_query($get_parameters);
}
```

Dave Olsen's Detector plus WURFL

With this approach we want to know all the details about HTML5 and CSS3 support that the Detector with its Modernizr test can provide us with, while at the same time we try to achieve the most stability and support for devices with little processing power. Throwing Modernizr into an old phone is useless as there is a high probability it may never finish loading. To avoid this situation, we assess a visitor's HTML capabilities by analyzing the UA string with WURFL. We use the `xhtml_support_level` WURFL property. When it is equal to or higher than 3, we include Detector; otherwise, we rely on the default screen width obtained from WURFL.

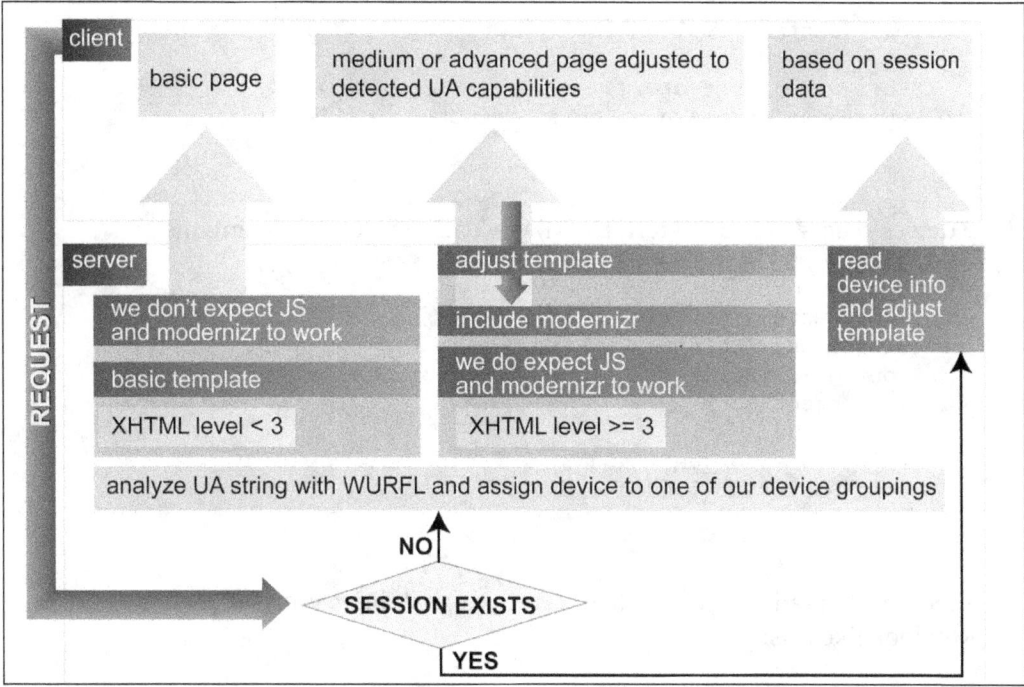

The implementation here is very similar to our first example except that in place of the cookie with the screen size we use Detector.

We start by loading the `wurfl_onsite` module inside the constructor, as shown in the following code:

```
function __construct(){
[...]
  $this->wurfl_object=getDDLobject('wurfl_onsite');
  $this->run();
}
```

Inside the `run` method, we use it to test for XHTML support, as shown in this code:

```php
function run() {
  $xhtml_level = $this->wurfl_object
    ->getDeviceCapability('xhtml_support_level');
  if ($xhtml_level < 0)
  {
    $this->device_class = 'unsuported';
  }
  elseif ($xhtml_level < 3)
  {
    $this->device_class = 'basic';
  }
  elseif ($xhtml_level >= 3)
  {
    $this->createDetector();
    $this->device_class = $this->detector_ua->family;
  }
}
```

If the device seems to use modern DOM, we load the Detector using the following code:

```php
function createDetector() {
  require_once ($this-
    >config['DETECTOR_API_DIR'].'Detector.php');
  if (is_object($ua))
  {
    $this->detector_ua = &$ua;
    $this->detector_loaded = true;
  }
}
```

The functions to read screen width and device capabilities with fallback to WURFL look like this:

```php
function getWurflWidth() {
  return $this->wurfl_object-
    >getDeviceCapability('resolution_width');
}

function getScreenWidth() {
  if($this->detector_loaded) {
    return $this->detector_ua->screenattributes->windowWidth;
  } else {
    return $this->getWurflWidth();
  }
}
```

```php
function getDeviceCapability($name) {
  if ($this->detector_loaded && isset(
    $this->detector_ua->$name))
  {
    return $this->detector_ua->$name;
  }
  elseif($this->wurfl_object->isCapabilityDefined)
  {
    $this->wurfl_object->getDeviceCapability($name);
  } else {
  return null;
  }
}
```

One of the things worth noting in the preceding code is the way we created device classes. It is not homogenous. If we use the WURFL capability `xhtml_support_level`, we set some device class name directly in the function body. But when we use `$this->detector_ua->family;`, the device, `family` or `class`, comes from the Detector library configuration in `app\libs\Detector\config\families.json` (as in the following snippet):

```json
{
  "tablet": {
    "isTablet": true
  },
  "mobile-advanced": {
    "isMobile": true,
    "features": [ "csstransforms" ]
  },
  "mobile-basic": {
    "isMobile": true
  },
  "desktop": {
    "isComputer": true
  }
}
```

Summary

We created four complete solutions to get a device's information from the libraries or via JavaScript object detection, store this information in a session variable, and read from a page or template. Based on those examples, you can choose the solution that best suits your needs — whether it is simple screen size detection, good support for low-end or older devices, or complete analysis of support for HTML5/CSS3 features.

In the following chapter we will take a closer look at the available solutions for handling adaptive images. We will also employ one of the modules created in this chapter to tackle the responsive images issue.

5
Responsive Images Client- and Server-Side Approaches

This chapter describes ways to deal with image scaling. With RESS, we can optimize the server-side part of our application in many ways depending on its target. But the issues discussed most often—related to SS optimization of RWD page components—are probably responsive images.

It is easy to add the following lines of code to a CSS file:

```
img {
  max-width: 100%;
}
```

This generally works. Most modern phones are able to resize a 3000px image to fit in a 300px wide screen, but it is neither a responsible nor a wise approach. Just think how much money it will cost your users. Mobile service providers love the pay-per-transfer plans. When 10 KB costs 2 cents, then 1Mb is worth $2, and that may be a waste for just a few unoptimized images. So, not optimizing images may bother your users in two ways:

- It makes them wait longer for your page to load
- It may cost them more money than it would for resized images

It's no wonder that this issue has gained so much attention, and is considered one of the most pertinent areas of concern in the development of RWD websites.

There are several concepts floating around:

- `.htaccess` redirects all `.jpg` files to adaptive images. It is the `.php` script that automatically resizes images according to the `$resolutions` configuration.

- `<picture>` tag with multiple `src` attributes — this is actually just a concept described in `http://www.w3.org/community/respimg/` and `http://picture.responsiveimages.org/`.

- Picturefill, available at `https://github.com/scottjehl/picturefill/`, is a JavaScript-based solution that mimics `<picture>` tag logic while using the currently available HTML5 tags.

- For Drupal implementations of this similar approach use the information available at `http://drupal.org/project/cs_adaptive_image` or view the formatter for Drupal available at `http://drupal.org/project/cs_adaptive_image`.

- Finally, we can easily use our four RESS receipts to serve image versions depending on the screen width. We can either use the screen-width parameter to automatically adjust image widths, or implement another system that would allow us to use other particular versions depending on screen size.

Scaling responsive images is not linear

Managing responsive images is more complex than relying on screen width. Scaling images is not a linear process, for the following reasons:

- Different screen widths often have a different column count

- Images may be cropped differently when being resized to fit different screen widths

The following figure shows how the scaling of images in RWD layouts is not linear:

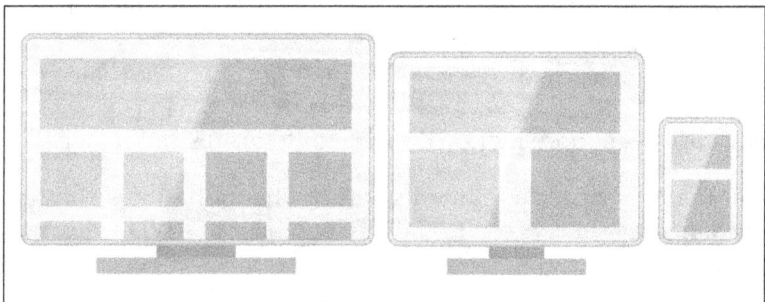

Scaling images in RWD layouts is not linear

Sometimes, as seen on the previous figure, on smaller screen widths, an image may appear bigger or equal to its size on wider screens. Also sometimes it is necessary to provide the image with different proportions or crop the image differently to keep it interesting in smaller sizes. The following figures show how plain scaling for lower resolution images doesn't work:

Plain scaling image for lower resolution doesn't always work.
Details become unrecognizable

The elements in the preceding figures, after scaling down, become hard to recognize. The same photo looks better in a smaller resolution after cropping it to a tighter composition.

Cropping image for lower resolution helps to focus attention on its subject

Plain CSS and Media queries – a solution with limited browser support

One of simplest solutions could be the **Cascading Style Sheets, level 2 (CSS2)** content property. With a code like the following:

```
@media only screen and (min-width: 501px) {
  img[src="img_front4_small.jpg"] {
    content: url("img_front4_big.jpg");
  }
```

It might be possible to replace `img_front4_small.jpg` with `img_front4_big.jpg`. The relevant images (defined by `content:` statement) are being downloaded by the browser only when the media query condition is met. The brilliant simplicity of this concept is dimmed by the following two facts:

- This is now only possible in Chrome, Safari, and Opera. In theory, content is a part of the CSS2 specification that is relatively old and widely implemented. This use case is a special one though and it is not well supported. The same applies to CSS `:before` and `:after` pseudo elements. Its wide support doesn't apply to the `img` tag.

- CSS is really handy when it comes to managing content versions. To make any real use of this method within a **Content Management System (CMS)**, with user generated content, one would have to create a framework that allows us to manage image versions easily.

The <picture> tag proposition

In 2012, some people created the Responsive Images Community Group in W3C Community and Business Groups (`http://www.w3.org/community/respimg/`) to create a proposal that adds new elements and attributes to the HTM5 specification. The intention of the proposal was to enable different sources of images, based on the browser and its display characteristics. An example of the `<picture>` tag might look like the following code:

```
<picture alt="">
  <source media="(min-width: 45em)"
    srcset="large-1.jpg 1x, large-2.jpg 2x">
  <source media="(min-width: 18em)"
    srcset="med-1.jpg 1x, med-2.jpg 2x">
  <source srcset="small-1.jpg 1x, small-2.jpg 2x">
  <img src="small-1.jpg">
</picture>
```

As of now, it doesn't seem likely that this will become a part of HTML5 any time soon.

Picturefill that mimics the <picture> tag behavior with HTML5 and JS

Picturefill is a polyfill (`http://en.wikipedia.org/wiki/Polyfill`) that mimics a proposed `<picture>` element using `<span>` or `<div>`. You can find it at `https://github.com/scottjehl/picturefill/`. To test it, we can use our sample site structure. After downloading a package from GitHub, I copied `picturefill.js` and `external/matchmedia.js` into our `/assets/js/` directory. Then I linked it from `RWD_sample_picturefill.html`, which is a copy of `RWD_sample.html` created in the first chapter. To link JavaScript code, just add the following lines of code:

```
<script src="assets/js/matchmedia.js"></script>
<script src="assets/js/picturefill.js"></script>
```

The file `matchmedia.js` contains the `matchMedia()` polyfill available at `https://github.com/paulirish/matchMedia.js/` for testing media queries in JS, and it is necessary to support the media attributes across browsers.

Now, I have to manually create images for each resolution and replace the following line of code:

```
<img src="assets/img/photo_big.jpg">
```

With the following snippet:

```
<div data-picture data-alt="Fall in przesieka">
  <div data-src="assets/img/picturefill/320_photo_big.jpg"></div>
  <div data-src="assets/img/picturefill/800_photo_big.jpg"
    data-media="(min-width: 400px)"></div>
  <div data-src="assets/img/picturefill/photo_big.jpg"
    data-media="(min-width: 800px)"></div>

  <!-- Fallback content for non-JS browsers.
    Same img src as the initial, unqualified
      source element. -->
  <noscript>
    <img src="assets/img/picturefill/photo_big.jpg"
      alt="Fall in przesieka">
  </noscript>
</div>
```

In the preceding code, we saw that the `<div>` tag with the `data-picture` attribute is a container for all image versions. The paths to images for each resolution are inside the `data-src` attribute of its child `div` elements. The `data-media` attribute contains a media query for each version. A similar pattern is used by `https://github.com/weblinc/picture`, and is based on the Drupal available at `http://drupal.org/project/picture`.

Drupal picture module screenshot

The preceding screenshot is a picture image module that relies on module **breakpoints**, and maps **image style** to **breakpoints** defined within a specific group. Both of those modules will be part of the upcoming Drupal 8 core.

There are several projects in Drupal that are focused on client-side responsive images.

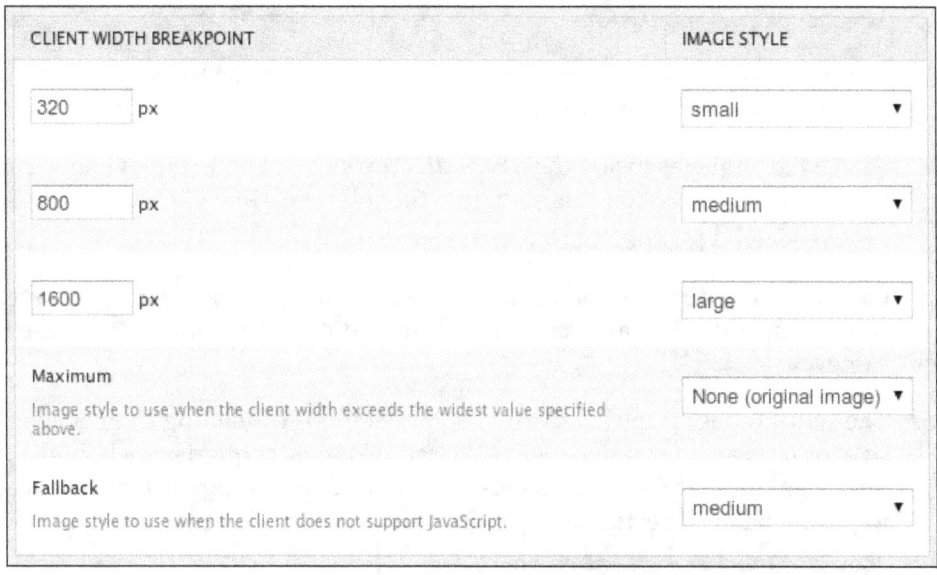

Drupal adaptive image module screenshot

The screenshot we just saw is from Drupal's client-side adaptive image module available at `http://drupal.org/project/cs_adaptive_image`. It allows for linking image styles with client width—obtained from the `document.documentElement.clientWidth` JavaScript object.

Automated creation of responsive images

We will take a closer look at the script by *Matt Wilcox*. You can download the recent version from the following website:

`http://adaptive-images.com`

This script relies on redirecting all requests for files (jpeg/gif/png) to `adaptive-images.php`. To use it, we need to set up at least three things:

1. Resolutions in `adaptive-images.php`—set values in the array as follows:

   ```
   $resolutions = array(1200, 800, 480, 320);
   ```

   This is the same as your media queries. Actually, you can add more if necessary. As we have media query stops only at 320px and 800px, I added 1200px and 480px, which allows for resizing full-width images to this resolution.

   Another variable in `adaptive-images.php` worthy of some thought is:

   ```
   $cache_path = "ai-cache";
   ```

   This sets the path for generating resized images and has to be specified relative to the document root.

2. As we have images inside the assets directory, we need to either comment it out in the file `.htaccess`, as shown in the following line of code:

   ```
   RewriteCond %{REQUEST_URI} !assets
   ```

   Or change the directory name. If we have any images we'd like to protect from being automatically resized, we can add respective directories here in same way.

3. The script relies on the JavaScript cookie method for reading client screen size, or uses an alternative method based on a media queries trick. In its documentation, there are two versions of JavaScript snippets that you need to put in the head section of your document. The basic version is as follows:

   ```
   document.cookie='resolution=
     '+Math.max(screen.width,screen.height)+'; path=/';
   ```

It is based on a slightly different approach than the JavaScript methods we used in the last chapter. It uses a `screen` object instead of `window`. In other words, it relies on the width of the monitor and not on the width of the window. In the case of a phone or tablet, the length is taken into account. The advantage of this approach is that the images served will be large enough for the widest browser window possible on a tested device. At the same time, one could say it is a disadvantage, as on a browsed page, in portrait mode, images will be wider than the browser window width. One could advocate the benefits of each of the solutions. For testing, it is easier to use `window.innerWidth` and see the changes after resizing the window, and reloading the page rather than having to change the monitor. We could use something like the following code:

```
document.cookie='resolution='+window.innerWidth+'; path=/';
```

There is another JavaScript version that takes into account `window.devicePixelRatio`. This property is implemented on Safari, Android WebKit, the current version of Chrome Android, the current version of Firefox, Opera Mobile, BlackBerry WebKit, QQ, Palm WebKit, and Dolfin. It depicts the relation between **Device Independent Pixels** (**DIP**) and actual physical pixels of the device. For example, the high resolution Retina display of a modern iPhone is equal to the value of 2.

```
document.cookie='resolution='+Math.max(screen.width,screen.
  height)+("devicePixelRatio" in window ?
    ","+devicePixelRatio : ",1")+'; path=/';
```

Finally, there is an interesting concept of using media queries to set a cookie without JavaScript. It uses the following CSS snippet:

```
@media only screen and (max-device-width: 479px) {
 html { background-image:url(ai-cookie.php?maxwidth=479); } }
```

And we can use a similar snippet for all necessary resolutions. To set the cookie via `ai-cookie.php`. This simple yet interesting concept to inform PHP about the screen or window resolution works pretty well in the current versions of major browsers. Some experimenting that show more consistent results, across browsers and hardware setups, are brought using `max-width` (window width) instead of `max-device-width` (screen width).

Versions of this script exist for C# and ColdFusion, as well as plugins for Drupal and Wordpress.

Server Side – using one of our example RESS systems

We will build a responsive image solution of our own, based on one of the samples created in *Chapter 4, Sample RESS Page*. The solution has the following aims:

- It should be able to serve images for any defined screen range.

- It should work with any image file format including transparent PNG.

- It allows for automated resizing with the possibility of manual override. The automated creation of images for smaller screen widths is a great feature, and indispensable in some workflows — like galleries with many images. On the other hand, in RWD layouts, it is better to optimize images for each resolution manually sometimes. This allows us to change proportions and focus our attention on an important part of the image, when we have limited screen real estate. Sometimes there should be different images for small screens, especially when there is text — banners and ads may be a good example.

Each of those aims has its advantages and disadvantages. We are now concerned mostly with the screen width for a particular template. We want the most accurate and up-to-date screen width we can have. These requirements are best fulfilled with the first and third solution from the last chapter — thanks to our custom cookie, which provides us with an updated window width with each request.

We will use the first approach, where we will rely on WURFL to create a fallback for devices with no JavaScript or Cookies. However, if we don't want this, we can switch to using our third approach with a pure JavaScript RESS receipt, by changing a single line in our page script in `ress_responsive_images.php`. Instead of the following code:

```
$RESS_obj = loadApp('ress_cookie_wurfl');
```

We can switch to a pure JS solution by writing the following:

```
$RESS_obj = loadApp('ress_pure_js');
```

 Pure JS solution can be found in the attached code file: `ress_responsive_images_pureJS.php`

But having this information is not enough. We will not provide image versions for every possible resolution. This just doesn't make sense — we have to decide how many versions are necessary and define resolution ranges for those specific versions. I prefer to use object interfaces for this, so instead of using the plain global variable $resolutions, I make a class Responsive_Images and set it up. The following code can be used to do the same:

```
$Responsive_Images = loadApp('responsive_images'); //this returns
instance of Responsive_Images class
$Responsive_Images->setResolutions(array(1200, 800, 480, 320));
```

What numbers should we put into this array? Our best guess is to start from where our media query stops, as it is, when the layout changes and we may need other image versions. But that is just a hint and it really depends on our layout.

Lowering the resolution of images does not always result in smaller images, as we discussed at the beginning of this chapter. For example, in our RWD page layout we reduced the number of columns at consecutive media stops. This causes images to enlarge as the screen width gets smaller. The simplest solution is to check for the nearest, biggest, or equivalent resolution:

```
$Responsive_Images->setScreenWidth($RESS_obj->getScreenWidth());
```

The preceding code informs the $Responsive_Images object what the current screen width is; we can then ask for the current resolution, that is, the lowest value in $Responsive_Images->resolutions, which is higher or equal to the screen width:

```
$Responsive_Images->getCurrentResolution();
```

The getCurrentResolution function, in the line of code we just saw after initial checks, creates a copy of $this->resolutions, and removes all values lower than the screen width. It continues to find the lowest values of what has remained or returns the string max:

```
function getCurrentResolution() {
  if (!is_null($this->current_resolution)) {
    return $this->current_resolution; // we already have it
  }
```

As we will use this function repeatedly, let's first check if we have this value already by using the following code:

```
if (is_null($this->screen_width)) { // we need screen width
  throw new Exception('first screen width has to be
    set with $this->setScreenWidth.');
}
if (is_null($this->resolutions)) { // and we need resolutions

  throw new Exception('first resolutions have to be
    set with $this->setResolutions
      or via config ["RESOLUTIONS"].');
}
$resolutions = $this->resolutions; // copy resolutions array
```

Delete resolutions lower than the screen width by using the following code:

```
foreach ($resolutions as $k => $val) {
  if ($val < $this->screen_width) {
    unset($resolutions[$k]); // remove smaller
  }
}
```

If there is no higher resolution in `$resolutions`, it indicates that we should use the original files; hence, we return max — that is, the name of the directory with the original images:

```
if (empty($resolutions)) {
  return 'max'; // we are in max resolution
}
```

Or we return a relevant resolution:

```
else {
  return min($resolutions);
}
}
```

I think that using directories to store image versions is more flexible than adding some prefix or suffix to file names. The following is the directory layout of our image library:

```
resp_images_root/max
  image1.jpg
resp_images_root/1200
  image1.jpg
resp_images_root/300
  image1.jpg
...
```

The `resp_images_root` directory needs to be set up either via `$config` in `app\` `responsive_images\conf.php`, or by setting it with the `$Responsive_Images-` `>setBaseImageDir($dir_name)` function variable. The path should be set as an absolute server file system path.

In the config file it looks like this:

```
$config['IMG_BASE_DIR'] = ASSETS_DIR . 'resp_img/';
```

You can see that we have used a new constant named `ASSETS_DIR`. It comes from global config (the one loaded via bootstrap):

```
define ("SITE_ROOT_FS", dirname($_SERVER['SCRIPT_FILENAME']) . '/');
define ("ASSETS_DIR", SITE_ROOT_FS . 'assets' . '/');
```

As assets are relative to the HTTP site root, I use:

```
dirname ($_SERVER['SCRIPT_FILENAME'])
```

To get site root directory which resides the page script requested by browser. Using function takes precedence over what could be set in the configuration file.

```
$Responsive_Images->setBaseImageDir(SITE_ROOT_FS . 'someotherdir/');
```

This directory should be accessible via HTTP, as we use file paths to serve images directly (not with PHP script, as it is in the case of the script by *Matt Wilcox*).

The `/max` directory holds the base versions of all images. Other (numeric) directories are for its derivatives. An image version is automatically created only when the two conditions are met; that is, the screen width is smaller than the image size and the derivative version does not exist.

To handle image resizing I used a third-party function available at `https://` `github.com/maxim/smart_resize_image`. I don't describe it here in detail as delving into PHP image handling functions is not the subject of this book. I applied to this function.

First, I changed the default argument values:

```
$proportional        = true,
// $output               = 'return', this is not necessary in my case
$delete_original     = false,
```

Second, I added `$targetfile` as a second argument to use it to output a modified image to file:

```
$output=$targetfile;
```

We only use this function to create a derivative file. The switch statement is used to select the output mode that needs to be commented out. You can find the modified function in the `app/libs/smart_resize_image.function.php` file.

The `getImage` function outputs the path to the image in a proper resolution for the current screen. It takes the `$filename` parameter, which contains the file path relative to the `assets\resp_img\max\` directory, that holds the original images. If the relevant image doesn't exist and the source image is wider than the current screen width, the resized version is created.

```
function getImage($filename) {
  if (is_null($this->base_image_dir)) {
    throw new Exception('first base_image_dir have to
        be set with $this->setBaseImageDir($dir_name)
        or via config["IMG_BASE_DIR"].');
  }
```

`$this->base_image_dir` needs to be set up before we do anything. If it is not set up, we throw an error:

```
  if(!$this->dirExists($this->base_image_dir)) {
    return false; // we should never get here anyway
  }
```

If it doesn't exist, the `$this->dirExists` function attempts to create it (actually not really necessary here, but if someone made a mistake let's make some use of it and create directory as a hint); the following code will check if the source image file exists:

```
  $image_source = $this->base_image_dir.'max/'.$filename;
  $img_file_exists = file_exists($image_source);
  if (!$img_file_exists) {
    throw new Exception('source file does not exists:
        max/'.$filename);
  }
```

If the source file exists, we build the path for a valid version. First, read the current resolution:

```
  $current_resolution = $this->getCurrentResolution();
```

Next, build a file system path for this file by using the following code:

```
  $dir_resolution_base=
    $this->base_image_dir.$current_resolution."/";
  $target_img_file = $dir_resolution_base.$filename;
```

And if it exists, we remove the SITE_ROOT_FS part of the path to get a path relative to the site root. If our site would get a more complex directory or HTTP path structure, we should probably build a full absolute HTTP URI.

```
if (file_exists($target_img_file)) {
  return str_replace(SITE_ROOT_FS, "", $target_img_file);
  }
```

In this way, we can always use the image we want to for every resolution. But if the source file resolution is smaller than the current screen size, we should return to the source file path, as shown in the following code:

```
$image_source_size = getimagesize($image_source);
$target_img_width = $target_img_file[0];
if(is_numeric($current_resolution)
  && $target_img_width <= $current_resolution) {
    return str_replace(SITE_ROOT_FS, "", $image_source);
}
```

If a file does not exist and the source image width is wider than the screen width, let's try to resize it and save it. First we analyze if the $filename parameter contains any directories, and if it does, we recursively create a whole directory structure in the relevant resolution directory:

```
$img_pathinfo = pathinfo($filename);
if(!empty($img_pathinfo['dirname']) && $img_file_exists)
  // target directory
  {
  if(!$this->iteratorDirExists($img_pathinfo['dirname'])) {
    return false; // we should never get
    to this point anyway
  }
}
```

Now we include the file with the code to resize the images:

```
require_once(LIBRARIES_DIR."smart_resize_image.function.php");
if(is_numeric($current_resolution)) {
  $res=smart_resize_image(
    $image_source,
      $target_img_file,
        $current_resolution); // target image width
  return str_replace(
    SITE_ROOT_FS,
      "",
        $target_img_file);
}
```

Passing three parameters to the `smart_resize_image` function is enough to achieve what we need.

To test this solution, we can use the RWD code from the first chapter. We should first move the images from `/asstes/img/` to `assets/resp_img/max/`. Then we use the HTML code from `RWD_sample.html` in `ress_responsive_images.php`. In all the image tags, we have to replace the actual path to the image with our function call. In place of:

```
<img src="assets/img/photo_big.jpg">
```

We can use:

```
<img src=
  "<?php echo $Responsive_Images->getImage("photo_big.jpg"); ?>">
```

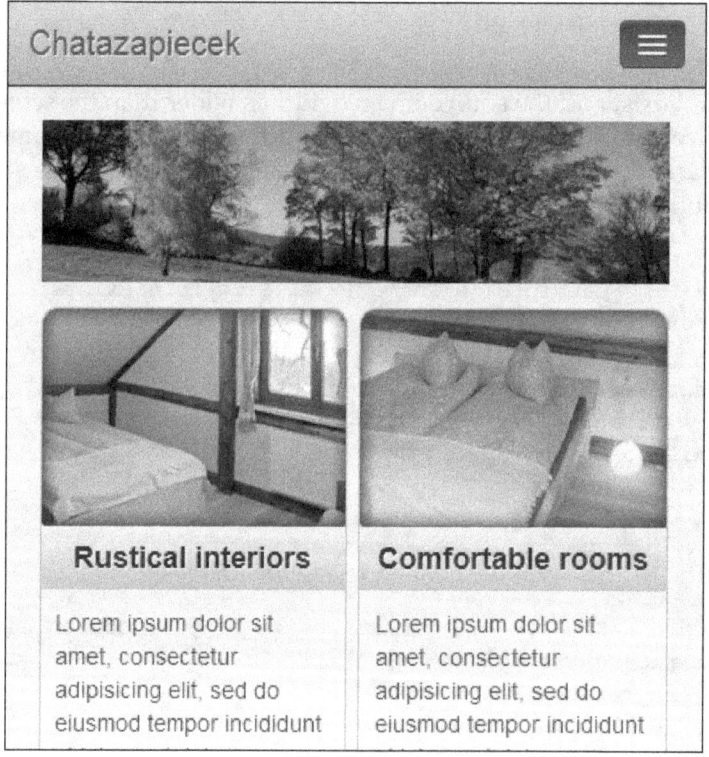

Our sample with all images scaled proportionally

The ability to manually override images for each resolution comes handy in situations like the one presented in the screenshot we just saw. All the images are nicely resized—in this case for 480px screen width—but the top image doesn't look proportionate. It would look better if it was cropped differently and placed a bit higher. Also, I used a certain trick that enhances the visual quality of a compressed .jpg while keeping its size relatively low. This can be achieved with maximum compression but also by oversizing the image. That's why I used an image that is 3200px wide as my base version, while actually targeting a 2000px wide monitor.

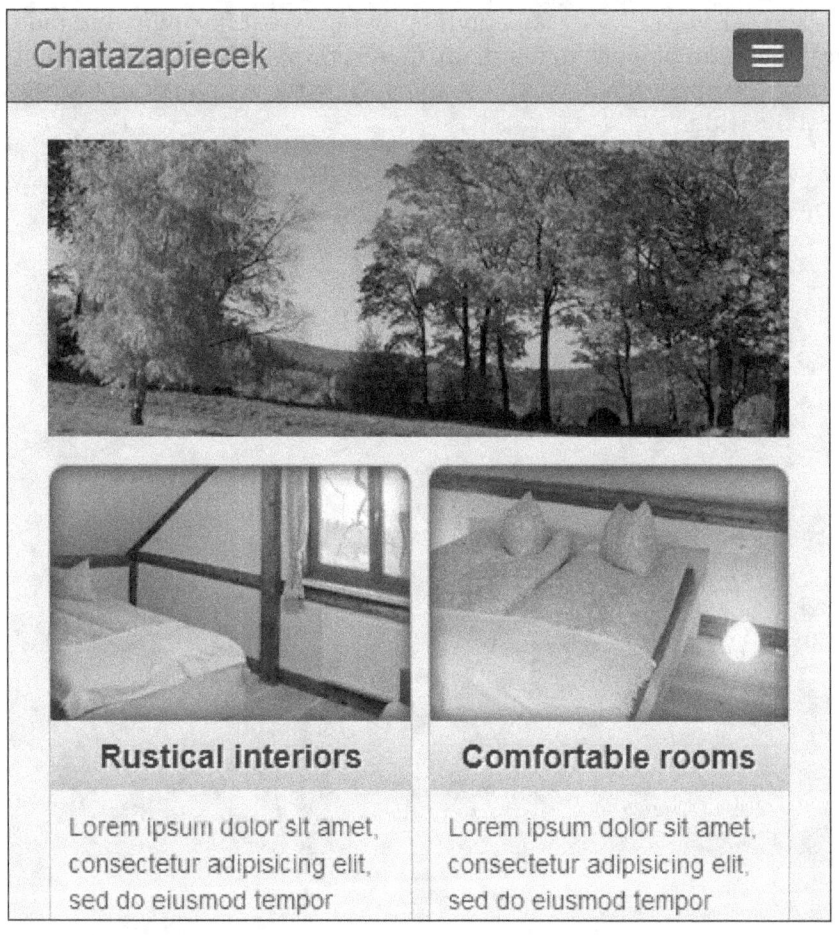

Our sample with top image cut in a way that suits overall composition better

The smaller images on the other hand, in a 320px to 480px screen width range, are a maximum 210px wide. After a manual resize from 480px to 210px, the files dramatically lose weight—from 20 KB/22 KB each to 5 KB/6 KB each approximately.

Summary

Among all the ways of creating and managing responsive images, each has its pros and cons. Aside from the purely technical aspects, such as reliability or compatibility, an important factor is, ease of use and flexibility. We usually gain one of those at the expense of the other. The concept from `adaptive-images.com` with `.htaccess` redirecting images to script and automatic generation of other resolutions is easy to set up and requires no effort to maintain. The disadvantage here is the inability to adjust the images manually for small resolutions and fine tune their size. The `<picture>` tag polyfill provides great flexibility but requires a significant amount of work to maintain. Our RESS solution is an attempt to create a balanced approach. It creates automatically resized versions but allows for manual override.

In the next chapter, we will discuss optimizing the performance of responsive pages. You will learn about optimization purpose, methods, myths, and limits.

6
Performance

Before talking about performance, we need to ask ourselves what this word means to us. Is this a real page-loading speed, the weight of the page and assets to be loaded, the page rendering speed, or maybe the largest number of devices to be compliant with?

Optimizing website towards screen size or bandwidth?

Adaptive Images optimization, which we did in the last chapter, was based on one parameter—screen width. With mobiles and modern devices, this might not be optimal. Just imagine someone using the new iPad (or another tablet with a large screen) with a weak 3G connection, or worse, GPRS with a pay-per-bandwidth plan.

That is why web developers would love to see bandwidth media queries. Knowing when the connection is made via low bandwidth would allow sending of extremely compressed images, while when the connection comes via a fast connection, we could serve the best quality we have. The problem is that bandwidth media queries "doesn't seem to be something that can be accurately implemented in the near future," as stated by *Yoav Weiss* in the article titled *Bandwidth Media Queries? We Don't Need 'Em!* in the Smashing magazine (available at `http://mobile.smashingmagazine.com/2013/01/09/bandwidth-media-queries-we-dont-need-em/`) after detailed analysis of how the TCP connections work. When he says "not in the near future," it looks like a cautious way of saying "never," unless maybe those biological computers in the far future make our understanding of networking obsolete.

For now the only solution to this dilemma (besides optimizing everything as much as we can) seems to be giving the user a choice between low and high bandwidth versions.

Optimizing images

Optimizing the use of images on a web page has the following five flavors:

- Optimizing image dimensions
- Optimizing image compression
- Optimizing the file format
- Avoiding the use of images
- Reducing the number of images

Optimizing image dimensions

Bitmaps have always defined dimensions in pixels. It is best when those dimensions match the exact area occupied by the image on the screen—without resizing with HTML or CSS. Scaling down images is possible only in the fixed layout of an HTML page. In responsive pages, fluid image scaling with CSS is a routine. We can only approximately adjust the actual image dimensions to its displayed size. We talked in detail about existing solutions in *Chapter 5, Responsive Images Client- and Server-Side Approaches*. The module `responsive_images` we created in that chapter allows adding image versions manually adjusted to each resolution. It has the following two advantages over purely automated generation (like the one used in the script from `www.adaptive-images.com/`):

- Usually most of the images used on the web page do not consume 100 percent of the window width. Hence using the window width as a determinant for every image results in leaving many of those oversized. Manual image-size adjustment for each defined resolution allows setting more precise image dimensions. This in turn gives a huge gain in bandwidth savings and page-load speeds.
- The `responsive_images` module allows manual fine-tuning of image compression.

Optimizing image compression

With Adobe Photoshop's Save for Web function you can interactively adjust compression parameters. "Interactively" is an important word here as proper optimization of compression parameters is an art of compromising between the file size and the perceived image quality. An interactive preview of the compressed picture allows swift selection of the best compression parameters.

 When saving in JPG format via Photoshop's Save for Web function, make sure to select either the **progressive** or the **optimized** option.

Optimizing the file format

Selecting the right file format is probably a well-known subject for most readers of this book. Nonetheless, there are some relatively new extensions worth mentioning too. Let's summarize the key points as follows:

- Images with a limited color palette (when the number of colors can be reduced below 256) are usually best saved as 8-bit PNGs (the additional gain is the lossless compression).

- Photographic images should be saved as JPGs.

- Remove metadata when saving.

- Don't embed a color profile.

- Use 24-or 32-bit PNG images only when you really need an alpha transparency or when the file size is smaller than the same picture saved as an 8-bit PNG/JPG (it happens in rare cases—especially with small files).

- Use fonts for icons—web fonts are well supported now in browsers. We can use fonts not only as letters but also as easy, flexible, and well-supported vector images. They can be easily scaled without losing quality and we can style them with CSS. An interesting source of free icons and a service that allows you to generate your own font is available at http://icomoon.io/app/.

Scalable Vector Graphics (SVG) is supposed to replace Flash in handling vector graphics for the web, and in vector-based animation. Currently though, there are no good tools for that and browser support is not consistent enough.

Avoiding the use of images

The CSS3 properties, such as border-radius, shadows, gradients, empower you to create many visual effects that were possible so far only with the use of bitmap images. If you don't know it yet, making rounded corners is possible now with a line of code. Tables filled with images died with dinosaurs a long time ago.

If I recently didn't encounter some "modern" dot NET components that position their stuff by putting tables inside tables and so on, I wouldn't even believe it's worth mentioning.

Reducing the number of images

With the CSS background-image position trick, we can dramatically reduce the number of HTTP requests (which is one of the basic factors determining the page-load speed). The basic use cases for this technique are hover images and icons. The idea is that you use one image for multiple icons or states, and change the `background-position` CSS property to show different fragments of this image to the user. Something like:

```
<div class = "icon clock"></div>
<div class = "icon mouse"></div>
withcss:
.icon {
  width : 20px;
  height : 20px;
  background-image : url("icons.png");
}
.icon.clock {
  background-position : 20px 0px;
}
.icon.mouse {
  background-position : 40px 0px;
}
```

Media queries optimization

It is easy to get fooled by myths about media queries optimization. For example, it is a myth that splitting CSS into separate files included via `@import` statements as follows, reduces bandwidth by loading only necessary CSS code:

```
@import url("479style.ss")screen and (max-device-width: 479px);
  @import url("767style.ss")screen and
  (min-device-width: 480px) and (max-device-width: 767px);
```

The truth is quite opposite. Such splitting of stylesheets into several files makes CSS easier to maintain but the browser downloads all the files. More HTTP requests certainly add overheads that slow down page loading.

Another myth I encountered is that all background images defined in a stylesheet are downloaded, even if they are inside media queries that do not apply to the current situation. That is not true. In the case of the following code, none of the major browsers download the `test1.jpg` image:

```
@media screen and (max-width: 800px)
{
   .photo_block4{background-image:url(test1.jpg);}
}
```

On the other hand, in the situation depicted by the following code the `test1.jpg` image is downloaded:

```
<div class="small">
  <imgsrc="test1.jpg">
</div>
```

The CSS applied here sets the `display` property to `none` on the element that is a parent of the image element:

```
@media screen and (max-width: 800px) {
   .small {display:none;}
}
```

The image is downloaded—probably due to the "so called" speculative parsing. When the browser encounters an image tag, it may immediately send a request for it—before it can know that it will not be necessary.

Testing

The fastest and easiest method is using the network panel in Firebug. Unfortunately, this is only good for testing on desktops. There are online services for testing the page-load speed available at `http://www.webpagetest.org/`. However, its methodology is undocumented and it is hard to rely on it when testing RESS applications. For example, in tests of pages built around the `<picture>` polyfill script (with iPhone 4 set as the target) the biggest images were always downloaded while with the RESS system in place during the first request, the smallest images were downloaded and during the second request the biggest images were downloaded. It seems that the WURFL screen width used during the first request returned 320 px, and the JavaScript later detected a large screen.

There is a widely advertised free mobile-testing tool available at `http://mobitest.akamai.com`. Unfortunately, we encounter similar problems in testing RESS pages as in the previously mentioned service. It tests only the first page load, which makes it quite useless to test every page that reads the screen width with cookies.

 The only method you can really rely on is testing your page on a device that is an assumed target or at least resembles it. To get some more insight, you may try the software available at `http://html.adobe.com/edge/inspect/` that allows simultaneous testing on several devices.

Nonetheless, using the network panel in Firebug provides valuable insights. The following figure shows a comparison of asset sizes in one of our RESS samples:

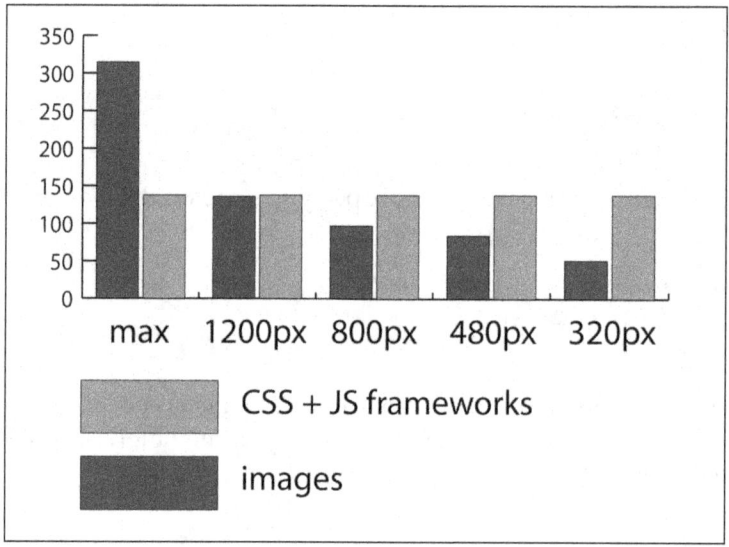

The figure shows a comparison of image and framework sizes based on the RESS example from the previous chapter. The CSS and JavaScript frameworks are Twitter Bootstrap and jQuery 1.10.2 minified. The file used in this example (`ress_responsive_images_pureJS.php`, attached to this chapter) should be placed in the same directory as `ress_responsive_images.php` from the previous chapter.

It shows that optimal image compression is not the only aspect of optimizing page-loading time. Our example is quite modest in image use. Nonetheless, the preceding chart is a bit surprising. Below 1200 px screen width, the CSS and JavaScript are bigger than the images, and most of this code is already minified (this is not an average — usually CSS + JavaScript is 30 percent of the image's size).

"Every day, more than 99 human years are wasted because of uncompressed content," writes Arvind Jain and Jason Glasgow in the article *Use compression to make the web faster* (available at `https://developers.google.com/speed/articles/use-compression`). Compressing HTML, JavaScript, and CSS can save a lot of bandwidth. The compression is not a developer's decision though. There are several factors that have to be fulfilled to make compression work. You can read more on this subject in the article at `https://developers.google.com/speed/articles/use-compression`. We can use a host with compression enabled (or enable it ourselves, for example, by installing Google's PageSpeed Module for Nginx or Apache from `https://developers.google.com/speed/pagespeed/module`).

While struggling to compress all resources to reduce the total transfer size, it'd be good to know what the actual value we should achieve is. There is no good KB number anymore. In the older times of modem connections, 50 KB was considered such a good value for a complete page with all assets. But it was simple due to similar connection parameters used by most of the Internet users. The difference between GPRS, 3G, HSDPA, DSL, T3, and 4GLTE connections used nowadays is huge. Generally speaking, more and more users are using some kind of a fast connection. It is reflected in the HTTP archive stats, showing a quick increase in the total transfer size of an average webpage (available at `http://httparchive.org/trends.php`) that reached 1585 KB on September 15, 2013.

However much transfer size limits seem to be virtually lifted for many Internet users, they do exist. Also increased complexity of JavaScript, new CSS capabilities, and growing image dimensions slow down rendering time. We are able to know neither the user's bandwidth, nor other constraints like his mobile data plan. These are good reasons to allow the user to select a lighter version of a website that he will receive by default.

Summary

We discussed ways to optimize the total web-page transfer size and the reasons to do so. It is a broad subject and a good starting point to learn more is to start using Google's PageSpeed Insights Browser Extensions (available at `https://developers.google.com/speed/pagespeed/insights_extensions`). Note that the versions for Firefox and Chrome work a bit differently, so it may be worth looking at both. Besides the ability to quickly review possible page-speed delays, it provides tips on how to speed up your page. One should not take those tips as a religion. For example, a standard tip we will see on each responsive page is "Specify image dimensions"—something that we definitely shouldn't do in this case.

In the next chapter you will learn how to create and use jQuery plugins, capable of turning elements of your page into interactive responsive components.

7
Extending with jQuery

With every month, more and more layout responsive patterns and responsive page components show up. The examples presented here show us how responsive plugins may help us solve problems commonly encountered when converting a website to a responsive design. Most of the responsive components rely on smart CSS but there are some that use jQuery plugins to improve usability.

Twitter Bootstrap components and plugins

In Twitter Bootstrap we already have several jQuery-based responsive components that we can use to improve navigation or enhance our page. A list of those may be found at `http://getbootstrap.com/components/` accompanied by a list of jQuery plugins that support them (available at `http://twitter.github.io/bootstrap/javascript.html`).

We already used responsive navigation in the first version of our page.

Let's implement a carousel. The new version of the script to customize Twitter Bootstrap allows us to use only the components we need. So far we didn't include carousel, so we have to download another Bootstrap version available at `http://getbootstrap.com/customize/`. On this page select **Carousel** below the **JavaScript components** label, **Carousel functionality** below the **jQuery plugins** heading, and the **Linked to components** label. Besides that, select the same checkboxes as we did in *Chapter 2, Sample RWD Setup for Client-Side Development*. Then go to the bottom of the page and click on **Compile and Download** to get our customized build. The downloaded archive contains two directories (CSS and JavaScript). Unpack it into the `assets/` directory (overwrite existing files if necessary). To see the working example, take a look at `RWD_sample_carousell_ok.html`. The downloaded CSS file should be linked inside `<head>` as follows:

```
<link rel="stylesheet" href="assets/css/bootstrap.css">
```

The minified Bootstrap JavaScript file we link at the end of file (to speed up page loading), just before closing the `</body>` tag looks like the following code:

```
<script src="assets/js/bootstrap.min.js"></script>
```

After the preceding line of code, we initialize the carousel plugin as in the following code:

```
<script type="text/javascript">
  $(document).ready(function(){
    $('#myCarousel').carousel()
  });
</script>
```

Before loading the `bootstrap.min.js` file, we need to load the jQuery too. The following line should be placed above the line loading `bootstrap.min.js`:

```
<script src="assets/js/jquery-1.10.2.min.js"></script>
```

Having the plugin and styles linked, we can start writing the HTML code of the carousel. It is described in detail on `http://getbootstrap.com/javascript/#carousel`.

We start from a `<div>` that will contain all carousel elements such as navigation, slides, and slide indicators. A good idea may be to use an `id` attribute to wrap the `div` class (as seen in the following code), so that we can later easily target the class from the script and use it in the `data-target` or `href` attributes of the navigation controls:

```
<div class="main_photo carousel slide" id="myCarousel">
```

The following ordered list creates circles indicating the current slide and allowing to navigate to any of them—note the `data-target` and `data-slide-to` HTML5 attributes:

```
<ol class="carousel-indicators">
  <li data-target="#myCarousel"
    data-slide-to="0" class="active"></li>
  <li data-target="#myCarousel" data-slide-to="1"></li>
  <li data-target="#myCarousel" data-slide-to="2"></li>
</ol>
```

The div variable of the class `carousel-inner` contains actual content for the slides, as seen in the following code:

```
<div class="carousel-inner">
  <div class="active item">
    <img src="assets/img/photo_big.jpg"></div>
  <div class="item">
    <img src="assets/img/photo_big_winter.jpg"></div>
  <div class="item">
    <img src="assets/img/photo_big_forest2.jpg"></div>
</div>
```

Finally, the code for the left and right navigation controls are as follows:

```
<a class="carousel-control left"
  href="#myCarousel" data-slide="prev">&lsaquo;</a>
<a class="carousel-control right"
  href="#myCarousel" data-slide="next">&rsaquo;</a>
</div>
```

To use this carousel with our RESS system from *Chapter 5, Responsive Images Client-and Server-Side Approaches*, we should only replace image URIs with a call to the `$Responsive_Images->getImage` method as follows:

```
<div class="carousel-inner">
  <div class="active item">
    <img src="<?php echo $Responsive_Images->
      getImage("photo_big.jpg"); ?>">
  </div>
  <div class="item">
    <img src="<?php echo $Responsive_Images->
      getImage("photo_big_winter.jpg"); ?>">
  </div>
  <div class="item">
    <img src="<?php echo $Responsive_Images->
      getImage("photo_big_forest2.jpg"); ?>">
  </div>
</div>
```

Responsive tables

Tables are one of the common challenges faced in responsive design. Dozens of columns will never fit in a 320 px screen width. Responsive patterns for table layout include:

- Converting a table into a pie chart (works only with numeric values). The test page for a plugin that converts the table to a chart can be found at `http://jsbin.com/emexa4`.

- Hiding several columns as the screen width is reduced. A jQuery plugin doing that can be found at `https://github.com/thepeg/MediaTable`, with an example at `http://consulenza-web.com/jquery/MediaTable/`. The great feature of this plugin is that it allows the user to control which columns should be displayed by selecting them from a drop-down menu.

Converting a table to an accordion element with jQuery

I selected this concept to show a way of creating responsive elements with CSS and some jQuery code. The plugin we are about to create in this chapter is inspired by the CSS-tricks example of reformatting a table with CSS into a vertical layout (as demonstrated at `http://css-tricks.com/examples/ResponsiveTables/responsive.php`). Our plugin will go a little further and will convert the table into an accordion type element. We start by stacking table cells vertically by converting rows, cells, and the table body to block elements inside the media query as follows:

```
@media screen and (max-width: 820px) {
  table.responsive td, table.responsive tr, table.responsive,
    table.responsive tbody {
  display: block;
  }
```

We don't need the column headers (with the field names) in the accordion, so let's hide those with the following code statement:

```
table.responsive th{
  display: none;
}
```

Instead of the `<th>` headers at the top of the table, we will add a field name to each row (this may sound cryptic but it should become clear when you open the file `table_responsive_sample.html` in a web browser and scale the browser window below 800 px width). To add a field name to each row (created from the `<td>` cell, replaced by injecting inline field names), we use the following code:

```
table.responsive td:nth-of-type(n+3):before {
    content: attr(data-col);
    margin-right: 8px;
    width: 30%;
    text-align: right;
    display: inline-block;
    font-weight: normal;
}
```

Injected field names are based on the `data-col` attribute value, which requires putting them in HTML as follows:

```
<tr>
    <td data-col="first name">Niki</td>
    <td data-col="second name">Doe</td>
    <td data-col="age">34</td>
    <td data-col="city">Paris</td>
    <td data-col="weight">70kg</td>
    <td data-col="hair">blond</td>
</tr>
```

This could be done directly in CSS by using the following code:

```
td:nth-of-type(1): before {
    content: "first column header";
}
```

The solution with the `data-col` attribute seems to be more flexible and easier to use, but that might depend on the use case.

We used `td:nth-of-type(n+3)` as we started from the third cell in a row. The first two cells contain the first and the second name. I'd like to put them in one line to be used as a header as in the following code:

```
table.responsive td:nth-of-type(1), table    .responsive td:nth-of-
type(2) {
  float: left;
  border: none;
  font-weight: bold;
  font-size: 20px;
  height: 28px;
}
```

first name	second name	age	city	weight	hair
Niki	Doe	34	Paris	70kg	blond
Alex	Jones	45	Austin	90kg	no hair
Jerzy	Kurowski	45	Przesieka	87kg	bold

Niki Doe   ⊕

Alex Jones   ⊖

age **45**

city **Austin**

weight **90kg**

hair **no hair**

Jerzy Kurowski   ⊕

Responsive table: it changes to an accordion type element below 820 px window width

To ensure proper layout we need to use clearing elements after each `<tr>` tag and before every third `<td>` tag as follows:

```
table.responsive tr:after {
  content: "";
  width: 100%;
  clear: both;
  display: table;
}
table.responsive td:nth-of-type(3){
  clear: left;
}
```

Use of the `nth-of-type` CSS pseudo-element is a great and simple way to differentiate between odd and even row styling, as seen in the following code:

```css
table.responsive tr:nth-of-type(2n+1) {
  background-color: #e4e2c0;
  border-top: 1px solid #f6f5e3;
  width: 100%;
}
table.responsive tr:nth-of-type(2n) {
  background-color: #ffecb3;
  border-bottom:1px solid #d9c496;
  border-top:1px solid #f6f5e3;
}
```

Add background and borders to complete the styling of the third cell and the following table cells that became rows, as seen in the following code:

```css
table.responsive td:nth-of-type(n+3) {
  background-color: #f8f2e5;
  border-top: 1px solid #fffbf2;
  border-right: 20px solid RGBA(255,255,255,0.3);
  border-left: 10px solid RGBA(255,255,255,0.3);
  font-weight: bold;
}
```

Now, as this is going to be an interactive element of the accordion type, we need some JavaScript. Ideally, we should be able to use it in a standard way as follows:

```javascript
$(document).ready(function(){
  $(".responsive").table2accordion();
})
```

To achieve the mentioned points, let's make a jQuery plugin using a standard pattern as follows:

```javascript
(function ( $ ) {
  var methods= {
    showRowCells:function() {
      return this.each(function() {
        //method code
      })
    },
```

```
      };
      $.fn.table2accordion = function(method) {
        if ( methods[method]) {
          return methods[method].apply(this,
            Array.prototype.slice.call(arguments, 1));
        } else if (typeof method === 'object' || ! method) {
          return methods.init.apply(this, arguments);
        } else {
          $.error('Method ' + method+ ' does not exist on jQuery.
    table2accordion ');
        }
    }) (jQuery);
```

 More on jQuery plugin design patterns can be found at
`http://docs.jquery.com/Plugins/Authoring.`

The `init` method (commented on in the following page) tells us the most on how
our plugin works. In the following code, we start by iterating each element in the
current selector and returning the processed element to preserve chainability. The
line `var $this, data [...]` allows easy access to plugin options.

```
      var methods= {
        init:function(){
        console.info("table2accordion.init");
        return this.each(function(){
          var $this = $(this), data =
            $this.data('table2accordion'); //standard construct
```

Continuing the `init` method call in the following code, let's hide all the cells starting
from the third cell in each row by calling the `hideRowCells` method. The line of
following code may seem a strange way to call a method inside a class. Nonetheless,
what is important is that executing the plugin method on the processed element
in this way allows us to receive proper object reference of the currently processed
DOM element in `$(this)` — instead of reference to some ancestor DOM element in
the current `$this`. In other words, we use the plugin chainability within the plugin
method, and at the same time it allows us to maintain chainability (as other ways of
doing this would limit the plugin's flexibility).

```
      $this.find("tr").table2accordion("hideRowCells");
```

In the following code we assign the click handler to the row:

```
      $this.find("tr").click(function(){
```

The `.data("opened")` variable is used as a flag indicating if a particular `<tr>` tag is in the `"opened"` or `"closed"` state, as shown in the following code, and depending on it relevant methods are called and the value of `$(this).data("opened")` is updated:

```
if(!$(this).data("opened")) {
    $(this).data("opened",1);
    $(this).table2accordion("showRowCells");
} else {
    $(this).data("opened",0);
    $(this).table2accordion("hideRowCells");
}
})
```

Actually, we could live without resizing the handler in most scenarios — usually the browser window is not being changed. But as we used the "max-width: 820 px" media query rather than "max-device-width", let's be consistent and at the same time provide a nice feature that demonstrates the layout change when the window resizes as follows:

```
$(window).resize(function(){
```

In the following code please note the method we use to check if a particular media query was applied. Instead of looking for the screen size, we check indirectly by looking at the CSS property. In our case `$this.css("display")` relates to `table.responsive ,table.responsive tbody{display:block;}`:

```
if ($this.css("display") == "block") {
    $this.table2accordion("turn2accordion");
} else {
    $this.table2accordion("turn2table");
}
});
})
},
```

The `init` method ends here.

The methods `turn2table` and `turn2accordion` essentially do nothing more than show or hide "data" table cells, as in the following code:

```
turn2accordion:function() {
    return this.each(function(){
        var $this = $(this), data =
            $this.data('table2accordion');
        if($this.prop("tagName") == "TR")
        {
```

Checking for `data("opened")` (as in the following code) allows some persistence. Scaling the window up and down leaves rows in the same "opened" or "closed" state they were in before.

```
            if($this.data("opened")) {
            $this.table2accordion("showRowCells");
            } else {
            $this.table2accordion("hideRowCells");}
        } else {
            $this.find("tr").table2accordion("turn2accordion");
        }
    })
},
turn2table:function() {
    return this.each(function() {
        var $this = $(this),
            data = $this.data('table2accordion');
        if($this.prop("tagName") == "TR") {
            $this.find("td:nth-of-type(n+3)").css({
                "display":"table-cell"
            });
        } else {
            $this.find("tr").table2accordion("turn2table");
        }
    })
}
```

The following methods, `hideRowCells` and `showRowCells`, do the actual work of hiding and showing "data cells" in a row:

```
hideRowCells:function() {
    return this.each(function(){
        var $this = $(this),
        data = $this.data('table2accordion');
        if(!($this.css("display") == "block" )) {
            return;
        }
```

Look for all the table cells and hide them using the following code:

```
$this.find("td:nth-of-type(n+3)").css({"display":"none"});
```

Accordion allows us to expand/collapse each row (it's not actually a row anymore as cells are stacked vertically; but because it is the HTML TR element, I still call it a row). To make our accordion more user friendly, we can show a plus/minus sign next to each header. Keeping the header look in sync with the row state (expanded/collapsed) is easily achieved here by swapping classes. If the TR element is processed at the moment, we remove the expanded class and add the collapsed class instead, as in the following code:

```
if($this.prop("tagName")=="TR") {
    $this.removeClass("expanded").addClass("collapsed");
}
```

Otherwise (as seen inside the else block in the following code), to perform this operation we have to first find the TR elements (rows) that are descendants of the current element.

```
else {
    $this.find("tr").removeClass("expanded").
        addClass("collapsed");
    }
})
},
```

The algorithm for showing rows is as follows:

```
showRowCells:function() {
return this.each(function() {
    var $this = $(this), data = $this.data('table2accordion');
    if (!($this.css("display") == "block" )) {
        return;
    }
```

But we show cells instead of hiding them, using the following code:

```
$this.find("td:nth-of-type(n+3)").css({
    "display":"block"
});
if($this.prop("tagName")=="TR") {
    $this.removeClass("collapsed").addClass("expanded");
} else {
    $this.find("tr").removeClass("
        collapsed").addClass("expanded");
    }
})
},
```

Adding and removing the expanded and collapsed CSS classes helps us in styling of the element, as seen in the following code:

```
table.responsive tr {
  background-image: url("../img/plus_minus_transp42.png");
  background-position: right 0px;
  background-repeat: no-repeat;
}
table.responsive tr.collapsed:hover {
  background-position: right -42px;
}
table.responsive tr.expanded {
  background-position: right -84px;
}
table.responsive tr.expanded:hover {
  background-position: right -126px;
}
```

As shown in the following figure, the image `plus_minus_transp42.png` (used as the `background-image` variable for `table.responsive tr` in the preceding code listing) contains all the versions of the plus and minus sign. Changing `background-position` is all we need to style the state of the accordion rows.

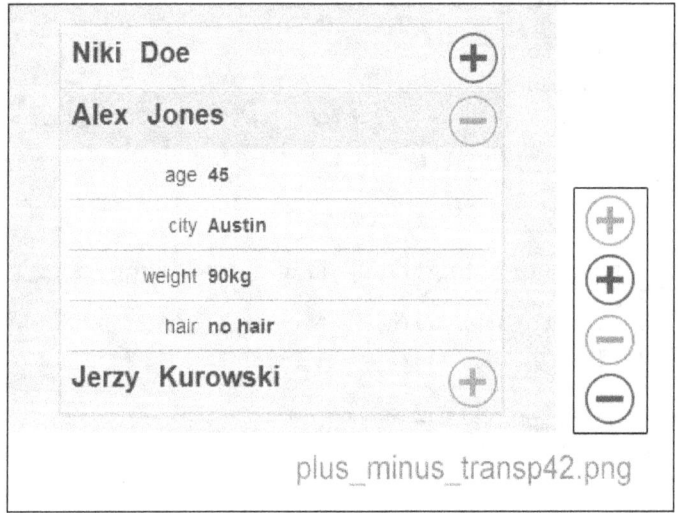

Styling with a single image

Masonry

Masonry is another jQuery plugin for a responsive, grid-based layout. It takes its name from positioning elements on a page such as "mason fitting stones in a wall". It represents quite a different approach to what a responsive layout is supposed to look and act like. Instead of scaling fluid columns, it repositions elements to best fit the page width.

It works best with designs based on a square module, but can be applied to other multicolumn setups too. Usually Masonry is used for designs where page building blocks repositioned by the plugin have a fixed size across all screen resolutions. Masonry can be found at `http://masonry.desandro.com/`. To use it, we only need to link the script `jquery.masonry.min.js` and initialize the plugin as follows:

```
<script src="jquery.masonry.min.js"></script>
$(function(){
$('#container').masonry({
  itemSelector: '.box',
  columnWidth: 100,
  isAnimated: !Modernizr.csstransitions
  });
});
```

In the preceding sample Masonry, we will use elements having the `.box` class that are descendants of the elements having a `#container` ID assigned. Additionally, the `modernizr-transitions.js` script is employed to animate boxes on the browser window size changes.

The following figure shows Masonry in action. The lower half is a screenshot of the page layout resized to 50% width as compared to the upper half of the image.

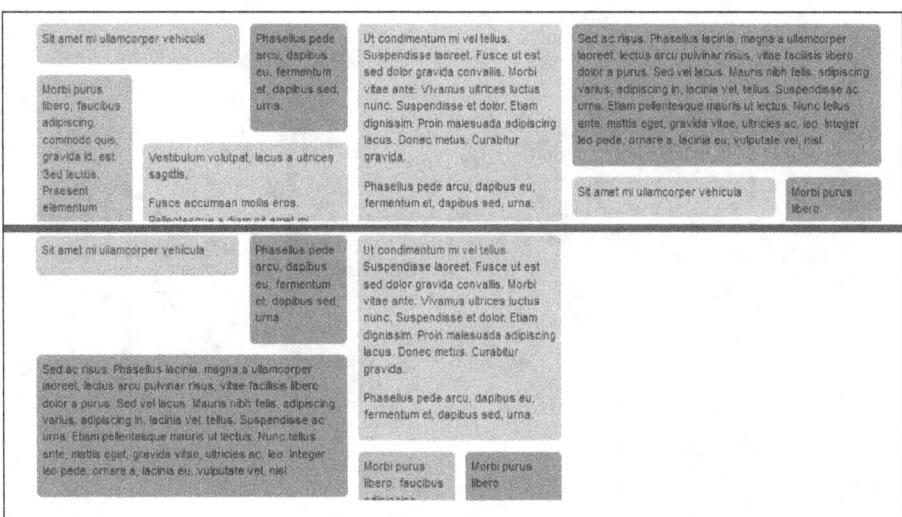

Summary

In this chapter we looked at the ways jQuery may help RWD layouts. We created a jQuery plugin from scratch, and employed another one from the rich library of Twitter Boilerplate components and plugins.

In the following chapter, we will create an AJAX application consuming RESTful API created with a PHP Slim framework. Then we will integrate it with our RESS responsive images module.

8
Employing a REST API for RWD

AJAX (Asynchronous JavaScript and XML) was invented to satisfy the need for a more responsive and functional web application. AJAX, by utilizing XMLHttpRequest, allows asynchronous exchange of data with a server to update parts of a web page without reloading the whole page.

 **XMLHttpRequest (XHR)** is a JavaScript API that allows you to make requests to a web server and load response data back to the script. Often, returned data is encoded in JSON format.

To build an AJAX application, we need some kind of API on the server side to respond to XHR. For some time now APIs inspired by the REST pattern are considered to be a good practice.

REST stands for "Representational State Transfer" and means an architectural style for distributed hypermedia systems. This concept was described in Roy Thomas Fielding's dissertation (available at `http://www.ics.uci.edu/~fielding/pubs/dissertation/rest_arch_style.htm`) written in the year 2000. During the last 13 years, "RESTful" has become a buzzword attached to nearly every modern web API. Fielding "frustrated by the number of people calling any HTTP-based interface a REST API" pointed out several rules that he deems required to call an API a REST API (available at `http://roy.gbiv.com/untangled/2008/rest-apis-must-be-hypertext-driven`) and insisted that everyone either "adhere to them or choose some other buzzword for your API."

REST is an architectural style described at a high level of abstraction. A RESTful web API is an API that uses HTTP methods GET, POST, PUT, and DELETE to perform operations on resources defined by a URL. For example, to read user information we can send the GET request to a URL like `http://test.com/user/2`, to delete the user we send the DELETE request to the same URL, and to replace existing user information with a new one we use the PUT method. There is more than this needed to make a web API a RESTful one. If you wish to learn more, take a look at the mentioned post by Fielding on REST and Hypertext.

It is relatively easy to add an RESS capability to AJAX applications as they already rely on client-server communication.

We will build a sample AJAX RESS application to manage landscape photos and allow different versions for different resolutions. Each photo has just two fields, country and location. We will give the users the ability to upload photos for each defined media query stop; if we don't upload an image, the application will generate a relevant file. The logic of managing photos is the same as in our RESS application from *Chapter 5, Responsive Images Client- and Server-Side Approaches* (folder `app/responsive_images`) and we will employ that module. Data will be stored in a MySQL database.

A simple single table like the following will do for our purpose:

```
'id' int(6) NOT NULL AUTO_INCREMENT,
'file_name' varchar(255) NOT NULL,
'location' text NOT NULL,
'country' varchar(255) NOT NULL,
PRIMARY KEY ('id')
```

 MySQL (`http://www.mysql.com/`) is part of the WAMP server mentioned in *Chapter 3, Server-Side Setup – Device Detection Libraries*. To create a database, start the WAMP server and go to `http://127.0.0.1/`. On the WAMP start page you should find a link to **phpmyadmin** under **Tools**. After clicking on it you are directed to a login page. You should use your MySQL password; if you didn't set it yet you should be able to login with the username `root` and an empty password. Upon login, create a database named `landscape` and load SQL from the file `app\rest_slim\photos.sql` (via the **import** tab in **phpmyadmin** — after selecting a database on the left). You also need to update the MySQL credentials in `app\rest_slim\conf.php`.

REST API

Our "RESTful" interface will consist of a few paths as follows:

- `GET /photos`: To load a list of all photos
- `GET /photos/:id`: To load photos and information
- `GET /photos/country/:name`: To load a list of all photos that belong to a country
- `GET /photos/countries/`: To load a list of all the countries
- `POST /photos`: To add a new photo
- `DELETE /photos/:id`: To delete a photo

Slim PHP framework and integrating the RESS module

We can use one of the many "RESTful" frameworks out there to speed up building our application. I decided to use Slim, available at `http://www.slimframework.com/`, for its simplicity. To integrate it with our framework, we put the Slim library into the `app\libs\` directory and load it from the `rest_slim` module. This module, consisting of the class `Rest_Slim` (in the `app/rest_slim` directory), will also load the `Responsive_Images` module and create database connections. The following constructor is responsible for creating the required environment:

```
private function __construct(){
```

First, let's read the configuration (as before) as follows:

```
include dirname(__FILE__)."/conf.php";
$this->config=&$config;
```

Next, we can load the Slim framework as follows:

```
require_once($this->config['SLIM_PATH']);
\Slim\Slim::registerAutoloader(); //register slim autoloader
$this->slim=new \Slim\Slim();
```

Create the PDO database connection using the following code:

```
self::$dbh = new PDO(
  "mysql:host=".$this->config['DB_HOST'].";
  dbname=".$this->config['DB_NAME'],
  $this->config['DB_USER'], $this->config['DB_PASS']);
self::$dbh->setAttribute(
  PDO::ATTR_ERRMODE, PDO::ERRMODE_EXCEPTION);
```

We need the `Responsive_Images` module too; in the following code we load the module using the path defined in `app/rest_slim/conf.php`:

```
if (file_exists($this->config['RESPONSIVE_IMAGES_PATH'])) {
  require_once($this->config['RESPONSIVE_IMAGES_PATH']);
} else {
```

If loading the module file fails, we throw an error as follows (error handling could be smarter but it's a lot of code for a short chapter anyway):

```
  die("module responsive images is required -
    check this path: ".$this->config
    ['RESPONSIVE_IMAGES_PATH']);
}
self::$responsive_images=new Responsive_Images();
```

The application will not work without knowing the resolutions for which we'd like to define image versions. In the following code, we pass the resolutions defined in the `app/rest_slim/conf.php` file to the `Responsive_Images` module:

```
if(array_key_exists('RESOLUTIONS', $this->config)
  &&is_array($this->config['RESOLUTIONS'])
  &&!empty($this->config['RESOLUTIONS']))
{
  $this->resolutions=$this->config['RESOLUTIONS'];
  self::$responsive_images->setResolutions(
    $this->resolutions);
} else {
  $this->resolutions = array(320); // fallback
}
```

Finally, we have to inform the `Responsive_Images` module about the current screen width. We get it from a cookie created in the same way as in *Chapter 5*, *Responsive Images Client- and Server-Side Approaches* but this time we read it with the help of the Slim framework as seen in the following code:

```
self::$current_screen_width =
  $this->slim->getCookie('screen_width');
if(!self::$current_screen_width ||
  self::$current_screen_width <= 0)
{
  self::$current_screen_width = 320; // some low fallback
}
self::$responsive_images->setScreenWidth(self::
  $current_screen_width); // set screen width - CRUCIAL
}
```

To avoid loading all these again and again, making this class a singleton (using the singleton design pattern) seems like a good idea (that is why the constructor is private here). To get an instance, we use a typical singleton getInstance method as seen in the following code:

```
public static function getInstance()
{
  if (!self::$instance) {
    self::$instance = new Rest_Slim();
  }
  return self::$instance;
}
```

Defining API with the Slim framework

With the environment ready, we can easily define our API with the Slim framework as seen in the following code:

```
public function setRoutes()
{
  $this->slim->get('/photos', array($this, 'getPhotoList'));
  $this->slim->get('/photos/:id', array($this, 'getPhoto'));
  $this->slim->get('/photos/country/:name',
    array($this, 'getCountryPhotos'));
  $this->slim->get('/photos/countries/',
    array($this, 'getCountries'));
  $this->slim->post('/photos', array($this, 'addPhoto'));
  $this->slim->delete('/photos/:id',
    array($this,'deletePhoto'));
}
```

Gateway file and path setup

The following code will be used in the gateway PHP file (ress_gateway/index. php), which can be placed anywhere provided we can put the .htaccess file to redirect requests and at the same time define a proper base path in the JavaScript of the application:

```
include "../app/bootstrap.php";
require_once(APPLICATION_DIR."rest_slim/app.php");
$app = Rest_Slim::getInstance();
$app->setRoutes();
$app->run();
```

To easily connect all the dots, we define the following methods:

```php
public function getGatewayUrl()
{
    return $this->getRootUrl().$this->config['GATEWAY'].'/photos';
}
```

The output of the preceding function is consumed inside the JavaScript code as follows:

```php
var rootURL = "<?php echo $this->getGatewayUrl(); ?>";
```

But we certainly can't call PHP from a `.js` file. We use the templates placed in the `app\rest_slim\assets\` directory — `ajax.php` in this case. Then this file is loaded using the following code:

```php
public function getJsApp()
{
    $ajaxAppPath = $this->config['MOD_ASSETS_DIR'].'ajax.php';
    ob_start();
    include $ajaxAppPath;
    $ajaxAppCode = ob_get_contents();
    ob_end_clean();
    return $ajaxAppCode;
}
```

Then we use it in the header section of our frontend file `rest_slim_test.php` (inside the HTML `<head>` element) as follows:

```php
<?php echo $app->getJsApp(); ?>
```

Implementing routes

To use the routes defined in `setRoutes()`, we call them using the jQuery `.ajax()` method as in the following code:

```javascript
function findAll() {
    $.ajax({
        type: 'GET',
        url: rootURL,
        dataType: "json", // data type of response
        success: renderMenu
    });
}
```

The preceding code is pretty much self-explanatory. The function findAll() called from the $(document).ready function loads the list of all the photos by sending the GET request to the /photos route and renders them using the renderMenu function. The PHP function getPhotoList() assigned to this route, reads all photos from the database as an array of stdClass objects, encodes them to JSON format, and sends them back using the following code:

```php
public function getPhotoList()
{
  $sql = "select * FROM photos ORDER BY location";
  try {
    $stmt = self::$dbh->query($sql);
    $photos = $stmt->fetchAll(PDO::FETCH_OBJ);
    //var_dump($photos);
    echo '{"photo": ' . json_encode($photos) . '}'; //here we send
JSON encoded data

  } catch(PDOException $e) {
    echo '{"error":{"text": ' . $e->getMessage() .'}}';
  }
}
```

On the client side, the renderMenu function receives this data in the data argument as seen in the following code:

```javascript
function renderMenu(data) {
  var list = data == null ? [] : (data.photo instanceof
    Array ? data.photo : [data.photo]);
  $('#leftmenu li').remove();
  $.each(list, function(index, photo) {
    $('#leftmenu').append('<li data-photoid="'
      + photo.id + '">'+photo.location+'</li>');
  });
}
```

The menu, when rendered this way, allows using the route /photos/:id to load the image for the current screen size. First we need to have the event handler attached to #leftmenu li as seen in the following code:

```javascript
$(document).on("click", "#leftmenu li", function(){
  getPhoto($(this).data('photoid'))
});
```

The click handler calls the getPhoto function, which builds the AJAX request as seen in the following code:

```
function getPhoto(id) {
  $.ajax({
    type: 'GET',
    url: rootURL + '/' + id,
    dataType: "json", // data type of response
    success: showImage
  });
}
```

The route /photos/:id is mapped to the PHP function getPhoto($id), as seen in the following code, which loads the file name from the database and translates it to the image URL in the relevant resolution with the use of the Responsive_Images module (we loaded this to the self::$responsive_images element in the constructor):

```
public function getPhoto($id)
{
  $sql="SELECT * FROM photos WHERE id=:id";
  try {
    $stmt = self::$dbh->prepare($sql);
    $stmt->bindParam("id", $id);
    $stmt->execute();
    $photo = $stmt->fetchObject();
    $picture_path=$this->getRootUrl().self::
      $responsive_images->getImage($photo->file_name);
    $photo->picture_path = $picture_path;
    echo '{"photo": ' . json_encode($photo) . '}';
  } catch(PDOException $e) {
    echo '{"error" : {"text": ' . $e->getMessage() .'}}';
  }
}
```

Please note that in the `Responsive_Images` module (loaded into `self::$responsive_images`) from *Chapter 5, Responsive Images Client- and Server-Side Approaches*, we use cookies and session variables. According to REST principles, the application state should not be stored or managed on the server (like session variables). Nonetheless, in our case cookie data is managed by the client and directly copied to the session variable for caching reasons. In other words, the application remains stateless between requests (stateless is referring here to the server itself).

Adding photos

These images are generated automatically when necessary, but we are going to allow the user to upload manually cropped images for each of the defined resolutions. To achieve this, we need to dynamically generate the file upload form. We will use the same technique as with the JavaScript code — with the PHP template included within the output buffer. The form template file at `app/rest_slim/assets/form_html.php` is loaded via the `getForm()` method into `rest_slim_test.php` using the following code:

```
<div id="form_wrapper" class="hidden">
  <?php echo $app->getForm(); ?>
</div>
```

Parsing the created photo form inside our class gives us the advantage of easy access to all class variables, as seen in the following code:

```
<h3>Create new photo</h3>
<p id="status"><span id="progress"></span></p>
<form id="landscape" enctype="multipart/form-data">
  <label>location</label>
  <textarea id="location" name="location"></textarea>
  <label>country</label>
  <input type="text" id="country" name="country" />
  <label>file for max width screen</label>
  <input type="file" id="photo" name="photo" />
<?php
```

In the following code, we iterate the `resolutions` array to generate the upload field for each resolution:

```php
if (is_array($this->resolutions)) {
foreach($this->resolutions as $resolution) {?>
  <label>file for screen width equal
    <?php echo $resolution; ?>px or less </label>
  <input type="file" id="photo<?php echo $resolution; ?>"
    name="photo<?php echo $resolution; ?>" />
  <?php }


}
?>
```

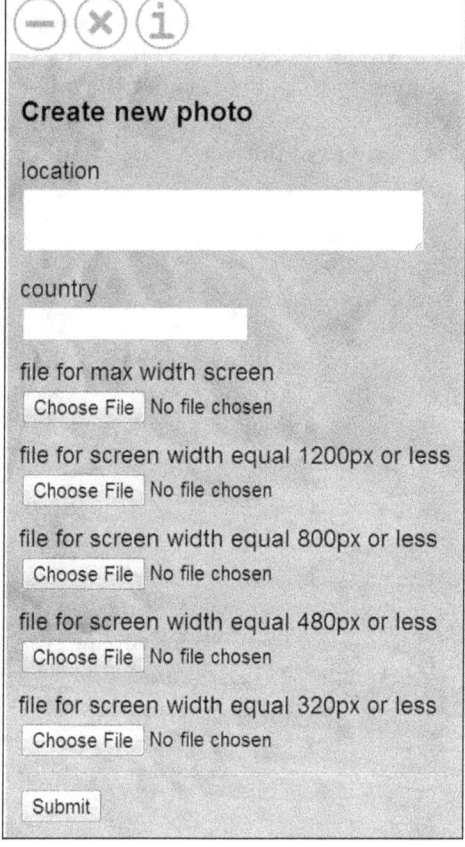

The create photo form allows uploading files for each resolution.

The following function, called upon clicking on the HTML element with `id="save"`, is supposed to upload files via XHR. It was impossible until HTML5 was used..

```
$('#save').click(function(){
```

We use the `formData` interface of XHR level2 as seen in the following code:

```
var formData = new
  FormData(document.getElementById("landscape"));
$.ajax({
  url: rootURL,  // same path as reading photo but with POST
  type: 'POST',
  xhr: function() {  // custom xhr
    myXhr = $.ajaxSettings.xhr();
    if (myXhr.upload) { // check if upload property exists
```

By adding an event listener, as in the following code, we attach the `progressHandlingFunction` to progress the event function handling of the file upload progress:

```
      myXhr.upload.addEventListener('progress',
        progressHandlingFunction, false);
  }
  return myXhr;
},
```

Then, upon success or failure of the upload, we display the pop-up boxes as follows:

```
success: function(data, textStatus, jqXHR) {
  alert('Photo created successfully');
},
error: function(jqXHR, textStatus, errorThrown) {
  alert('addPhoto error: ' + textStatus+errorThrown);
},
```

The form data to be uploaded is as follows:

```
    data: formData,
    cache: false,
    contentType: false,
    processData: false
  });
});
```

We need to use similar processing on the server side in the addPhoto() method mapped to POST /photos as seen in the following code:

```
public function addPhoto() {
  $req = $this->slim->request();
```

First we process the file for max resolution using the following code:

```
if (array_key_exists('photo', $_FILES)
  &&$_FILES['photo']['error'] == 0) { // we got file

  $filename = $_FILES['photo']['name'];
```

We rely on the directory structure implied by the Responsive Images module as seen in the following code:

```
$base_images_dir =
  self::$responsive_images->getBaseImageDir();
$target=$base_images_dir."max/".$filename;
move_uploaded_file($_FILES['photo']['tmp_name'], $target);]
```

Then we iterate $this->resolutions to the build form field names again, and save the uploaded files to relevant the directories using the following code:

```
foreach($this->resolutions as $resolution) {
  $form_field_name = 'photo'.$resolution;
  if(array_key_exists($form_field_name, $_FILES)
    &&$_FILES[$form_field_name]['error'] == 0)
  {
    if(is_dir($base_images_dir.$resolution)) {
      move_uploaded_file($_FILES
        [$form_field_name]['tmp_name'],
        $base_images_dir.$resolution."/".$filename);
    }
  }
}
```

Getting the form values via a request object from the Slim framework can be seen in the following code:

```
$location = $req->post('location');
$country = $req->post('country');
```

And finally, we insert the record into the database using the following code:

```
$sql = "INSERT INTO photos (file_name, location, country)
  VALUES (:file, :location, :country)";
try {
  $stmt = self::$dbh->prepare($sql);
  $stmt->bindParam("file", $filename);
  $stmt->bindParam("location", $location);
  $stmt->bindParam("country", $country);
  $stmt->execute();
} catch(PDOException $e) {
  echo '{"error": {"text":'. $e->getMessage() .'}}';
}
}
}
```

There are two key points in the preceding example presented as follows:

1. It shows how to create a RESTful API and an AJAX application that uses it.
2. It demonstrates integrating this application with our RESS solution.

What is it good for?

Some say that REST "will power the future of the Internet" (http://www.phparch.com/2012/02/what-will-power-the-future-of-the-internet-rest-or-soap/). For several years we have been able to see the constantly increasing significance of client-side programming and the evolution of APIs powering them. PHP programmers cannot ignore this trend as it already influences the leading PHP frameworks, such as Symphony. Let me quote Fabien Potencier (http://fabien.potencier.org/article/49/what-is-symfony2):

"I don't like MVC because the Web has evolved a lot in the recent years and some projects are much different than the projects we had some years ago. Sometimes, you just need a way to create a REST API. Sometimes, the logic is mostly in the browser and the server is just used to serve data (think backbone.js, for instance). And for these projects, you don't need an MVC framework."

So the simple answer could be that learning this pattern of building web applications is good to better understand where web programming is heading. In particular, it may be useful for creating smart and fast administration interfaces, for extending existing systems with flexible RESS capabilities, and for creating websites that immediately respond to user actions, something that was once called Rich Internet Applications (http://en.wikipedia.org/wiki/Rich_Internet_application).

Summary

The sample application created in this chapter demonstrates how an AJAX application using the RESTful API created with the Slim PHP framework can be easily extended to include RESS features, such as responsive images. To test this, a MySQL database has to be created; the loaded SQL from `app/rest_slim/photos.sql`, and the database configuration in `app/rest_slim/conf.php` has to be updated too.

Index

U

UA string
  analyzing, with WURFL 59-61
UK Digital Cabinet Office blog
  URL 8
users 11, 12

W

WampServer
  URL 33
web page
  testing 85-87
website
  image, optimizing 82
  optimizing 81
window.devicePixelRatio property 71
WURFL
  UA string, analyzing with 59-61
  using 46, 47
  versus DeviceAtlas 32
WURFL Cloud version 39, 40
WURFL file
  downloading with PHP API, URL 33
WURFL library 33-37
WURFL_WURFLManagerFactory
      instance 37

X

XMLHttpRequest (XHR) 103

Z

ZURB CSS Grid Builder
  URL 14

**Thank you for buying
RESS Essentials**

About Packt Publishing

Packt, pronounced 'packed', published its first book "*Mastering phpMyAdmin for Effective MySQL Management*" in April 2004 and subsequently continued to specialize in publishing highly focused books on specific technologies and solutions.

Our books and publications share the experiences of your fellow IT professionals in adapting and customizing today's systems, applications, and frameworks. Our solution based books give you the knowledge and power to customize the software and technologies you're using to get the job done. Packt books are more specific and less general than the IT books you have seen in the past. Our unique business model allows us to bring you more focused information, giving you more of what you need to know, and less of what you don't.

Packt is a modern, yet unique publishing company, which focuses on producing quality, cutting-edge books for communities of developers, administrators, and newbies alike. For more information, please visit our website: www.packtpub.com.

Writing for Packt

We welcome all inquiries from people who are interested in authoring. Book proposals should be sent to author@packtpub.com. If your book idea is still at an early stage and you would like to discuss it first before writing a formal book proposal, contact us; one of our commissioning editors will get in touch with you.

We're not just looking for published authors; if you have strong technical skills but no writing experience, our experienced editors can help you develop a writing career, or simply get some additional reward for your expertise.

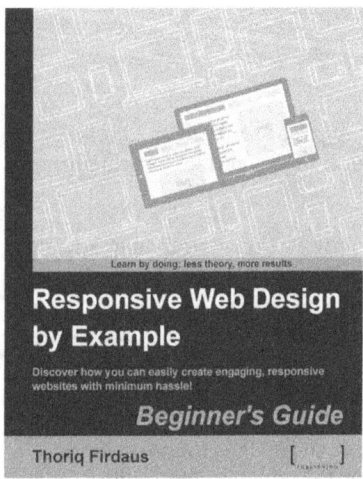

Responsive Web Design by Example

ISBN: 978-1-849695-42-8   Paperback: 338 pages

Discover how you can easily create engaging, responsive websites with minimum hassle!

1. Rapidly develop and prototype responsive websites by utilizing powerful open source frameworks.

2. Focus less on the theory and more on results, with clear step-by-step instructions, previews, and examples to help you along the way.

3. Learn how you can utilize three of the most powerful responsive frameworks available today: Bootstrap, Skeleton, and Zurb Foundation.

Instant Responsive Web Design

ISBN: 978-1-849699-25-9   Paperback: 70 pages

Learn the important components of responsive web design and make your websites mobile-friendly

1. Learn something new in an Instant! A short, fast, focused guide delivering immediate results.

2. Learn how to make your websites beautiful on any device.

3. Understand the differences between various responsive philosophies.

4. Expand your skill set with the quickly growing mobile-first approach.

Please check **www.PacktPub.com** for information on our titles

Responsive Web Design with HTML5 and CSS3

ISBN: 978-1-849693-18-9   Paperback: 324 pages

Learn responsive design using HTML5 and CSS3 to adapt websites to any browser or screen size

1. Everything needed to code websites in HTML5 and CSS3 that are responsive to every device or screen size.

2. Learn the main new features of HTML5 and use CSS3's stunning new capabilities including animations, transitions and transformations .

3. Real world examples show how to progressively enhance a responsive design while providing fall backs for older browsers .

HTML5 and CSS3 Responsive Web Design Cookbook

ISBN: 978-1-849695-44-2   Paperback: 204 pages

Learn the secrets of developing responsive websites capable of interfacing with today's mobile Internet devices

1. Learn the fundamental elements of writing responsive website code for all stages of the development lifecycle.

2. Create the ultimate code writer's resource using logical workflow layers.

3. Full of usable code for immediate use in your website projects.

Please check **www.PacktPub.com** for information on our titles

C D PYBUS

ATHENA PRESS
LONDON

ISBN 10-digit: 1 84401 944 6
ISBN 13-digit: 978 1 84401 944 1

First Published 2008
ATHENA PRESS
Queen's House, 2 Holly Road
Twickenham TW1 4EG
United Kingdom

Printed for Athena Press

Foreword

The writing is on the wall. Not many read it. Fewer try to understand it. But when you do, it tells an important story; important because it makes what is usually seen as 'senseless and mindless' meaningful and relevant in this climate of terrorism; important because it tells us something different about society's folk devils – the teenage male.

@ Mass Fear attempts to analyse and also give voice to one of the most demonised yet pure means of street art – graffiti. Graffiti is a way of building masculinity, communicating power and independence, being a 'nobody' and becoming a 'somebody'. This book is the story of the intimate and private thoughts of Calvin – a 'somebody' – and a must for any council, school principal or anyone interested in graffiti.

This is a story of the interior and unrecorded. It tells the story of lives and experiences that leave little or no textual record, no documentation on which a scholar can base a thesis. It also touches on the history of the so-called 'losers' rather than the powerful ones, giving voice to those unremarked women and men who slide into the dark and leave scarcely a trace of their passing.

@ Mass Fear presents the personal story and a cultural project in which the search is for insight into our common humanity, for insight into what used to be called the human condition. When Calvin began to work on writing his story from memory and as the experiences of his life began to come together in one place, it became clear to me that in writing his own story he was telling pieces of stories of other people who had touched our lives as well. These stories include the childhood heartbreak felt across different working class families who, often because of economic necessity, split up. In Calvin's case, as a little boy who had to be an adult before his time, he and his brother were sent from Flinder's Station in Melbourne to Sydney. Struggling not to cry alongside his younger sibling, Calvin was an image of bravery to his mother when he arrived in Sydney a man.

There is really no common denominator among graffitists except their shared story. Graffiti is all about people. It's about relationships, and individuals and motives. They can be rich or poor, they can be of ethnic descent or not, highly religious or from an entirely secular background. They tend to define the common purpose of their group existence as defensive and for friendship and tend to 'stick up for each other' in contrast to many Aussie youth.

They are, however, generally all-male groups. While a central activity of the groups in graffiti is to paint 'tags' and achieve fame amongst friends, meeting, watching and attempting to impress girls are also prime objectives, so there is usually no way that girls can actually belong to the group or 'crew'. This subculture is a site for masculine construction; in fact, male graffiti writers marginalise and exclude female writers and, with this, their emasculating threat. I have felt this ever since I started painting in the eighties, being female and always the 'outsider'.

There are many books written about the graffiti underground but this one opens up the doors of its secret masculine universe. It describes how the battle of graffiti centres on a fight for power and control of the underground scene. Although writers do not and will never literally control this, they use their graffiti as a symbol of domination. The authorities' failure to keep their trains or walls free of graffiti is taken to signify the subculture's supremacy.

Graffiti's rewards are manifold, but there is a thread connecting them. Put together, they articulate a process of change and development, transitions and progression. Like the Boy Scouts, this subculture could be viewed as a modern-day 'rite of passage'; a transitional vehicle which helps many male members journey from one status to another. They enter as a boy and a 'nobody' and, having completed its tasks of endurance and fed off its rewards, they emerge a man and a 'somebody'.

These stories include those of some of the most influential figures belonging to the pioneers in the Australian graffiti world. Some of the stories in @ *Mass Fear* also remind me of Diego Rivera and Frida Kahlo who each had a distinctive style to their art yet their works conveyed their view of the world and themselves. For me it is painting. Since I was a young girl I have dreamt I was flying and in my imagination my flying machine is an old paintbox with home-made wings. I keep my tools in my pocket: a spray gun, a can, a pencil camera and a mouse. Inside the paintbox are colours and pictures and ever-changing collages of the things that inspire me, but I always fly from my house to walls of caves through to streets and motorways. Calvin's art – his poetry and battle raps – decrypt a way of life that remains mysterious to many: the life of the 'artist'.

This book represents an artist writing about creativity. It talks of the messiness of artistic creation that is common across painting, literature, poetry, graffiti, music and film. Indeed, there is a great deal about art that is also messy in the literal sense, as well as clumsy, awkward and blunt. And because it is hard for those who write about art and artists to know what to say about these aspects of the process, they ignore them or try to clean them up.

Because most people cannot read the letters of graffiti, they cannot understand the reasons for such writing. It is, in fact, repeated exposure to names or 'tags' which seems to inspire a new writer's interest. 'Each person has their own tag, kind of like a logo in advertising, and it was the logos of those names I was initially inspired by' (Futura 2000, one of the most famous graffiti artists who began his career in the seventies). In recognising these names, new writers begin to recognise the point of the subculture fame. As the graffiti-covered walls and surfaces of the city act as a form of subcultural advertisement, this is also a place where naïve, new writers can be recruited by underground groups other than just hip hop. These tags provide a goal for new writers, and inspiration to develop 'the individual genius'. They indicate and set a standard for what can be bettered and it is also this which feeds the competitive spirit of the subculture.

One of the points of this book is to show that being an artist really does involve setting out and suffering the consequences of one's dreams. The consequences, it scarcely needs to be pointed out, are often unpleasant, even if not in a life-threatening way. The license artists grant themselves is potentially socially destructive.

Calvin has captured the essence of the concept that choosing to be an artist involves putting oneself on the line in a way that many people have trouble understanding. Graffiti remains one of the few cultures unchanged by the rise and proliferation of cultural prizes and by our economy of mainstream cultural production and prestige. With mainstream art beginning to resemble sport, with its roster of winners and losers and its spectacles of competition, its ties with celebrity, commerce globalisation and media, graffiti is still pure. There are tens of thousands of anonymous artists painting today whose cultural capital goes unperceived and undervalued and whose currency, in reality, grows stronger with each new piece they paint. Such public art is criminalised and passes unacknowledged in our economy of false prestige.

It seems to me that one of the reasons we are so keen to puncture the myth of graffiti and the individual creative genius is that we do not wish to think too hard about what is involved in being an artist. We are at once humbled, threatened and mystified by the priapic egoist that is the barrel-chested, Y-fronted Picasso; similarly with the bearded Matisse with his pigeons and paper cuts, or the Van Goghs who cut off their ears; similarly with those who wear their backward baseball caps and paint on trains or commit suicide or, like Brett Whiteley, turn to alcohol or drugs or suffer nervous breakdowns. The list today, like yesteryear, is endless. Well, it is all a shame, but if one really must turn into a cliché, so be it.

'What the artist creates in imagination is, as a rule, what he is debarred from actually living,' wrote Stefan Zweig in *Casanova*. Certainly, the tension between interior, creative life and exterior, 'normal' life is a great source of conflict in any real artist's life. Graffiti is often the hidden secretive recreation of an often ordinary-looking teenager whose 'real life is often a model of sobriety and sanity.'

The contribution this subculture makes in modern Australia, if not in the world, cannot be underestimated. Finding a meaningful route to adult/manhood is not an easy task for young people today. Material resources like money or a career are not yet accessible or relevant and traditional avenues via public displays of physical prowess or bravery are all but obsolete. In this day and age, the young have to be a little more creative and find ways of building their own props and operating their own rites and rituals to find their identity and their own cliché.

As @ *Mass Fear* states, this subculture provides us with a wonderful example of this creativity, which is centred in building nationalism. It can take willpower – great selfishness or great sacrifice – to resolve the inner conflict, or any resolution is unlikely to be lasting. Whilst more people than ever claim to be artists, few experience deeply the tension between their inner imaginings and their outer life as graffiti writers do.

In 1901, the very first Nobel Prize for Literature that set the modern prize train for culture in motion, was won by the Frenchman Sully Prudhomme. One of the unlucky losers that year was Leo Tolstoy, who wrote *War and Peace* and *Anna Karenina* and who never won the prize. Instead, Sully Prudhomme, the author of... (well, you tell me!) won. Life is short but art can be long indeed, with or without prizes. Just like graffiti.

Dear News Editor...

Please report the other side:
Graffiti genocide,
As decided by the misguided.
Ask Mitre 10 in the city
About graffiti being bad for
Business.

Or is it not mentioned
'Cause no one asks the
Question? Well!

Are top-of-the-range
Spray cans on sale from the
Prime front of their city
Outlet for profit?

Or is it a shop front for
The undercovers?

Either way, the paint sold
There rarely gets used for
Legals.

Business sells on the back
Of this culture.

And that's why talking is
Just that.

After all, we are so busy
Saving the world in a
Diplomatic way

With our UK
& USA buddies.

Who also have graffiti
Concern, just ask the
French.

We seem to be running a little
Slow on this one, it
Started 30+ years ago.

During the time of the
Vietnam war, street
Vandalism was up too.

The objectors are not
Defectors. They only run with
The freedom we allow.

'Freedom's just another
Word for nothing left to
Lose' – Kris Kristofferson.

You can't find the answer if
You don't know what the ?
Is.

Melbourne Sin-Herald have
Not printed the attached
Letter, emailed to them.

They have run a week-long
Feature on the subject and
Had a poll on punishment.

Only to end up with less
Than 1,500 responses at near

60% for, 40% against
Harsher laws.

Without once in that week
Reminding themselves of
The government project
That had a young
Graffiti writer doing good
In the community with some
Kinda DVD project
In-schools
After a stint doing some
Work on *Home and Away*.

How wonderful, a role
Model with the make-up
Already on. How soon we
Forget. The anti-terror laws
In Australia detained this
Young man
Only months ago, as it is
Said he was planning with
Friends to hurt Australia.

Very James Bond: so, like, I
Know! It's Top Secret and
That's why they overlooked
This little
Piece of recent
International history.

Who's da crim?

This is a time for our
Peoples to come together
And start with positive
Ways of being.

It's a shame this won't go
To print.

Don't want to upset
The advertisers, do we?

Cal I-_-I

From: Phantast
To: news@heraldsun.com.au
Sent: Friday, January 20, 2006 7:46 p.m.
Subject: FW:

If u r receiving this for the first time it might seem messed up. Please b understanding that the letter to the Herald-Sin in Melb'n was in response to a feature they have been using for the last week that in my opinion is not in the best interests of our people.

PPE (Passenger of Planet Earth)

----- Original Message -----

Hi Jen. You must be in another world to the one I live in. 16 years in this culture – that's an asset to our community.

Eye 4 Eye

That's how it was written. **war** and its declaration has impacts on the minds of all Australians. John Lennon asked me 2 imagine.

So... In the town of Beenleigh there was such a declaration made against one graffiti writer. He is now **dead** – died before he could vote. With a rope around his neck after painting an illegal piece 4 his girl. I saw this young Australian in the afternoon as he jumped from a youth worker's car, ran across 2 me with his usual lateral dialog putting words in your mouth. Asking if he could do a piece as we were packing up a demo 4 the Fox art show going on inside the Logan Art Gallery. His family life was poor; his energy needed nurturing. Did someone write that about Adolf once? Maybe they should have! I believe that the word **war** is a very strong one, that will cause greater division in our community of Australia. And it is for this nation & its future, I say, 'Shut your eyes, it might help you see, that by your actions you are pushing Australians against one another in a time we really don't need the underground forming alliances with people who find extreme ways of declaring **war**.'

I'm now going to send this E 2 da PM.

If u go
With flow
U will say what u know.
It ain't really smart
To throw that dart
With lies and hatred in our heart.
You may as well just fart,
'Cause that ain't art
It's war!

Cal I-_-I
lll

From: Phantast
To:
Sent: Tuesday, January 31, 2006 10:20 p.m.
Subject: Fw: some if could of red this wood 'av changed tit tit it

Hi,

Really like the Hitler story, hope we never forget Hitler was a rejected artist. In the past we look not to make the same mistakes. Please add criticism to my words. We are trying to write a book here! It might help me see what it takes to debate a subject in your media. Stopping believing in what we are doing is not an option.

By the way, someone rang saying they were from channel 7, heard my ramble for a bit and said they would speak to their boss. They have got back to me.

Singer.

Cal I-_-I
lll

From: Phantast
To:
Sent: Wednesday, January 25, 2006 11:18 a.m.
Subject: graff

Hi,

Melbourne was the city of my birth in 1961. My name is Calvin and I live in Queensland now. I left Melbourne in 1972. Sydney was my home until 1982 but the QLD Gold Coast has been my home since. I took my family to Melbourne for Xmas this year. We spent time with relos, as you do. Swam in Bass Strait & the Yarra. On Boxing Day we drove to the TV towers on the ding/de/dongs, where more relos live, and which overlooks the Silvan View Dam.

This is a place as a child of ten years old I had explored. We lived in Mooroolbark. My family was a broken one and us four kids (aged 5, 9, 10 and 11) were sometimes left to fend for ourselves for a few days. On one occasion, my brother, one friend, one dog (Nipper) and I, took on the Mount Everest of our childhood and climbed the face of the ding/de/dongs, pulling our dragsters up with us. So many times we looked down and thoughts of giving up were becoming a real option. Something kept us going though. Perhaps it was the thought of the view from the top or the realisation that we could do it or maybe the ride down the hill (which was the reason for the adventure in the first place) which drove us on.

After a short rest on top of the world as we knew it, we glided down the road with the breeze whizzing past and a smile you can only imagine 2b in a Disney film. At the bottom of the hill we waited for Nipper, our loyal mutt. We were all glowing like never before in our lives, looking back to see if Nipper was coming.

Then, just as we were thinking we might have to send out a search party for him, Nipper came around the last bend towards us, limping. His paws were bleeding from trying to keep up with us on the road surface. If only we had planned ahead, we could have explored many options to avoid the pain of knowing we didn't consider holistically our action. (Nipper was OK, he was a tough little nugget.)

Graffiti has been a big part of my life for more than sixteen years. I have a few questions:

1. How many years has Melbourne been planning for the Commonwealth Games?

2. How many years has graff covered the man-made structures in the pretty city of Melbourne?
   a. 5   b. 15   c. 25+

3. How many countries coming to compete will have their eyes burnt out from seeing graffiti?

4. How many people remember Brisbane's Commonwealth Games and the clean up before that did not end graffiti in that city.

5. How many people walk quietly past a hornets' nest? How many hit it with a stick, hoping that will make it go away, only to end up with multiple stings, wishing they had spent more time planning.

Please don't declare war on our own, spend more time planning. Nipper left enough blood on our man-made streets. We have got the answer underway and have a book coming out soon that will offer an option for bringing the writers and wider community together. It is the result of sixteen years of working with the international subculture known as hip hop.

Cal I-_-I
lll

From: Phantast
To:
Sent: Friday, February 03, 2006 10:57 p.m.
Subject: hi

Haven't had a chance 2 finish that book yet. It's like something keeps exploding every time I turn. Lots of illz in this house of mine. You remember my speech at 29 Palms? Well, it's now time to come together and represent! With the date here 2-day 2 × 3 = 6 and where u r it's 3 × 2 = 6. As great as **life** is for the many Passengers of Planet Earth dudes, it can be better for all. (PPE) 2 × 3 = 6 minus 2 days.

Walk a while in my shoes & that of the people I meet. Walking in our main city mall with a PPE another PPE who stood out in the crowd by sitting down with bags of plastic scattered around with all the PPE's worldly goods in them. (**Art: the other address is my Uncle Bill, methinks u 2 would get along.**) PPE waves me towards him, reaching towards one that would have magic possessions inside. Why else would PPE carry it around? Leaning towards this PPE, he shuffled as he was in a hurry to get the content out. He handed me 2 sticks that were burnt at both ends. Clapping them together, he said so very softly, 'You can play them with your didge!' Well, I was carrying one at the time! I received this wonderful gift, went 2 shake PPE's hand only 2 b shown a palm and the sound of **HOW**. I returned the greeting and continued up the mall, acting like a monkey, when I saw a spray can artist painting another fridge magnet. We *need* more fridge magnets. More visual stimulus for our young who have been in conflict with **the man** for more than 30 years. Sorry, paths blurring 2gether. (**Art: u will be happy @ knowing that of all the people i told that story 2, Uncle Bill was the first one to tell me what i already knew, that i had received a gift form the richest ppe in da city.**)

Went to visit Bill at Xmas just gone. He lives in Melbourne Victoria, Australia. Melbourne is the host city for this year's Commonwealth Games. This will all make sense later, but 4 now it's back 2 da big picture. This world we *live* in has carried this PPE 2 this day. And I've got something 2 say! Or is it pray?

Now a flesh from the newsdesk:

The shareholders of Planet Earth are all =.

That concludes our news 4 ever. Now you gotta bleaf on sumsting young laddie. Sounds like the incorrigible, the one and only Mr Peter File. They only know love them kids, like dat's all day got. Please don't tack dat away from 'em. Goingoooooooffffffffffffffffffffffffff.

Meanwhile back 2 da task at hand: tomatoes and fridge magnets.

> We can grow
> Many tomato.

And so the guests move in and own what they want. Sometimes they want what we need, so we are killed and kill for our love-need.

European

I'm a European, I'm a European.
I'm the worst thing this
World has ever seen.
I'm a lean, mean, destruction
Machine
I've always been keen
To be seen
As the one who's conscience
Is so fucking clean.

I'm a European, I'm a European.
I'm the worst thing this
World has ever seen.
After fighting with
Ourselves for endless years,
We jumped on our ships to
Spread our fears.
We'll rule this world with
Our gods & guns
And we do this in a quest for funds.

I'm a European, I'm a European.
I've got a standard of living
That's filled with strife.
It shouldn't get confused
With quality of life.
The sky, the land & the sea
I'll pollute,
Just to get my hands on some
More loot.

It doesn't matter if I beg
Or borrow;
Got to get it now,
stuff tomorrow.

I'm a European, I'm a European,
The worst thing this
World has ever seen.
I'm so smart,
I can fly to the moon.
The way I'm stuffing up this
Planet, I might have to live
There soon.
The world will continue to
Suffer the scars
Because there are decisions
Being made by men leaning
On bars.

I'm a European,
the worst thing this world
has ever seen.

KFC 1992

```
        n n
         n
        mmm
```

My 1st techno skull.

Strange feeling when u 'ave spirit guides. Don't know if I will use this? See how we feel about it later. Tired now. Mussssssssssssssssssssssssssssssssssssssssssssssssssssssssssssst not stop. We must sing 2 1another! And boy do I got singing 2 do! Is it this way 2 heaven or this way 2 hell? We all gotta story 2 tell.

15 kms

So I'm a kangaroo
Hopping down the road.
'Yo!' Shit, just squashed
A cane toad!

So here I am in the middle
Of the street,
Standing, staring at the
Poison on my feet.

Looking up, I knew I was
Out of luck.
Over the hill came a
Mac truck.

From the truck there came
A noise, it sounded like a trumpet
With a roo bar on the front;
I didn't want to bump it.

'Yo, here's no place to stand!'
No way was this my intention;
I don't want to die from
Human intervention.

Life's no computer game –
It can be full of strife.
There's no pause, revival,
Bonus round.
Just one shot to make
A good life.

Time had come to make a big
Decision.
5 more seconds and I would be
In this prick's rear vision.

Truck was so close
I could hear the driver's brass.
Got 2 get this trumpet-blowing
Baboon off my arse.

Tail's up! Come on legs,
Time to start pumping!
Started hitting the road so
Hard it sounded like thump'n

Passed a dingo named Jesus;
He wasn't moving fast.
Told him to get a move on or
His next move would b his last.

As I went through town
I was jumping over cars;
Jesus went under them,
Banged his head,
Started seeing stars.

As the truck ran over him
There was quite a splatter.

1 less dingo in the world –
Does it really matter?

You may have got his body
But you'll never get his soul;
This dingo named Jesus
Had reached his final goal.

Almost out of town
McDonald's at the end of the street;
Could have died right there.
No! I can think of better things to eat!

Truck was so close
I could hear the trumpet blowing
Wondered what sort of load
This prick was towing.

So I asked a brolga,
To check it with haste
He circled round once
Then told me 'toxic waste'.

What the shit! This guy's an
Environmental disaster;
Driving like a maniac across
This land I once did master.

Over the sound of the truck
I could hear a kookaburra.
This was the last sound
I ever heard.
15 kms from Bingara.

C P 1989

World Expo: 88

The buy-centennial tear. Well, the missus was the most popular artist on site: (insert prequel). Who knows, Star Wars did it successfully. One year later we have two art co-ops. Lots of craft too. Enter PPE.

'Hi! Really like the airbrushing. Who does it?' asked PPE.

'The cheese and kisses,' I reply. 'What you and da other PPE doing?'

'We're doing a break-dance show in the mall. Just warming up in here. It's OK isn't it?'

'Sweet. Might come and watch. Missed a lot of the shows at World Expo: 88. Working all da time. So you like the missus' work?'

'Yeah, we paint with cans,' PPE replied. 'We'd like her to teach us how to colour with air and light like she does with her spray.'

This seems to start off an adventure like that would take till now to begin to complete, when that bitch, June, said, 'We got a video camera. Let's go video some graffiti stuff.'

I said, 'We can ask why these guys aren't supported like in a club.'

She wanted to know how to help them and my idea of a club was ideal. It's so long ago it's hard to remember but that was the start of **art clubs**. I feel like I must go on sow sow sows owsowsowoosowosowosow.

> Reap rhymes with sleep.
> Morning has almost shocked
> The hell out of me.
> Maybe it's the sounds, the cool,
> The colours (**that's color art**).
>
> Time 4 a spel cheque.
> We have discovered a new
> Language, can you read it?

Some say the driver's liver
Was fried,
Some say it was murder –
Suicide,
And Dodi and Di died.
The graffiti – what does it say?
PPE = Passenger of Planet
Earth.

The teachers struggle with
The kids who don't all
Turn out of the same fridge
Magnet factory.
'How many 6s in 23?' Mr Crosby asked
The children in his class
As we painted a mural
For them all outside their
Class.

1,2,3,4,5,**6**,7,8,9,10,11,12,13,
14,15,16,17,18,19,20,21,22,23.

'I'm right! You only have 1, sir!
1, sir!'

Flashback

PPE walks into public toilet. Two PPEs, same sex, leave in a big hurry, adjusting clothes as they head towards their rides. One of those rides being bestowed with the rego 'Oi, sir!' PPE in the back of the car asked whether or not they were up to sumting, to which I replied, 'That PPE still got half a mongrel.'

Sex has no gender. PPEs have survived this shock to their lives in principal. Moments before this free gay porn act, we had all driven past the faces wall on the highway. 1 km long, 4.5 metres high, it took four years to finish. 1,000 helped, 190 children's faces appear on a minimal background (it would make a great fridge magnet, serious). And this has been the tale of two who never knew what it was really like to be down with this sort of social behaviour before. Shocked they were!

Graffiti can educate our children, even in the eyes of the blind. We need to get lateral children spending time with stimuli that can hold their attention, instead of disrupting others who seem to have less going on in their heads. The special needs of creative lateral PPEs may be undressed/address; we can nurture these creative minds and if they don't sell out to the industrialists, we may have used our brains and not our bucks to address our quality of life. (**Those burnt sticks sit on my left: multibiotootheatermusical.**) Yes, I'm making it up as we go wherever. Download from Down Under! Hope this ain't spinning anyone out. Please, if it becomes too much, just go walkabout. Saw that movie in high school – all boys except the teacher. Balgowlah cinemas 1974ish. Sweet. Now that's going way back. Thank you brave educators. Walkabout was the name of this film and also the term used to describe a spiritual journey undertaken by the male of the tribe upon this great southern land. A lot more fun than English classes. And now, jolted by the sand at Byron Bay today, trying to do a handstand before entering the surf, we're back to the quack to have an X-ray on the left shoulder. See what I meant at every turn? It's 1989 again. PPE, June & I road-trip the east coast of Oz. First stop: Sydney.

> My father lives in Sydney
> You know,
> It's that town that had that
> Olympic show.

My father, my father...
(yes, this is taken from an unfinished song I wrote).

In Sydney 1989, we all meet PPE who shows much compassion for the youth and allowed a wall in his car park to become a hall of fame for writers. He also showed how his adventure into NASCAR races in the States inspired the movie with Tom & Nicole, *Days of Thunder*. No long-term solutions were offered, but we must thank PPE for the leg of lamb and the time we received. Time waits for no lamb, so into the f-truck and off on our 600 mile (old-school kilometres) quest to roast the lamb at uncle PPE's place in Melbourne to cook the sucker, (**was delish**). Melbourne exposed more than we bargained for, with a transit officer doing an interview with us whilst forgetting to zip his pants. We also met PPE who did allow minimal graffiti to be done while the budget lasted. When that budget ran out the limited writers engaged would be offered alternatives, like candle-making, tie-dying stuff, underwater basketweaving, get it! Thank god they weren't the type to teach kids to swim, then take the water out the pool.

Don't think this was the holistic approach we were hoping these two biggest cities of Oz would have in place. Well, it was in the Dark Ages, after all. The internet was some way off keep your stockings from falling down at that time. Mobile phones were the size of house bricks and the youth of this nation were starting their new way of making the people notice the freedoms we all enjoy. Graff in Oz was almost ten years old. Mags, clothing, cans from the USA and Europe were marketed by the youth. June and I have been spoken highly of in such mags, maybe cause we are concerned enough.

PPE's are in sync with the street
And the people they meet,
So if u can't compete
Please take a seat!
Time 2 get 2 my feet,
Dis rhyme is complete.
What an amazing feat,
Neat beat. 'Bleet
Bleet bleet,' said da man.

Upon our return to our home state we enquired as to po-lice (ref: attached photo) strategies in Queensland,(**yes, Art, this is the name of the state I live in**).

We visited the big po-lice station in the city and did an interview with a Mr Wall (po-lice officer), who had run a couple of legal walls to see if this approach to the rapidly growing culture would meet the demand. It seemed like there was a supply and demand imbalance that still continues to this day. Fame was there to be had by the few who had this opportunity to develop skills with the law on their side and free paint to boot. Some of this free paint would also end up in the boot (trunk?) of the cars to be used later for after-hours activities! It seemed no one really was looking hard enough to come up with the answer that could give a long-term solution with all parties being happy.

The adventure paused due to a bad case of timing. I was involved in a near-death experience. Three wannabe noms who weren't wanted by any bike clubs thought I had just rolled this dude for four Gs. So, as you do if you are one arsehole ×3, you try to kill people for their money. This sure stacked some shit in the closet that needed some time to get out. These freaks went on to kill someone weeks after fucking me up. Sad, sad story as the victim was about to become a father for the first time after just coming into money and moving to the big smoke with a brand new Harley-Davidson for his ride. I felt guilt for his child-to-be and his bride.

The day of the murderers' court appearance, our trusty/rusty van was burnt in the driveway outside our bedroom window. My mind shut down.

It was time 2 hide and regain some pride.
June was the glue and knew what 2 do.
I'm as 2 as 1 can b.
U c, it's not all up 2 me.
Will return after brainbettergets.

If you guys are reading this, please pass comment as guts are spilling here to hopefully leave our youth in less conflict with our law-makers. If I have written something that has not been explained well enough for you to understand, I would like to make it all good. I'm not even sure you would want to follow this and feel I have thrown this at you. It is the way I would like to continue if you don't mind. I feel like I'm telling a story to my uncle Bill and Art at the same time and somehow that comforts me.

If you were to delete the last message as the next one comes in this would free up a lot of space. It would also make me feel more certain that the story we tell (June and I) is being told to elders who can see our adventure from that perspective. I don't know how this sits in your lives now and if it isn't still well, I hope things get better soon.

Two chiefs, the young Indian and squaw, have return to tell of their adventures.

Hang on a minute. When did we send these two out? 1989–2006. What happened to that two-week turnaround you promised?

In 1989, the year after Expo: 88, June and I started a new gallery in Surfers Paradise. Mainly her spray art paid the rent. We won Australia's Costume Character of the Year Award in Wollongong (south of Sydney). The strange mayor stole my keys whilst standing talking to me in the street. What a sleight of hand this man had. He didn't mind using this trick on at-risk youth, who ended his life for him. Kids grow up in many different ways, the ones with this sort of scaring rarely seek revenge. (Frank should have learnt to wank: possible new rhyme about the crime!!!!!)

Whilst shopping with daughter we noticed some new items in the toy section. Hip hop limbo was one.

1989 returns with the let's-make-graff-video story. Must have been a somewhat normal year for someone out there. Not for this little red duck.

June has a daughter from a previous relationship. This young one was spending a lot of time with her gran, while June was trying to get her art out there, taking her message to the streets after a violent end to this coupling that had produced a kid. He, the ex, suicided in 1988. A hole was dug and he was gone before I could meet him. I did however speak to him once on the phone, letting him know that it was my intention to stick with this relationship for ever. We soon moved into Beenleigh as I had come from a broken family and knew how it was to lose constant contact with the ebb and flow that is family. There we had an old house to move into, a legacy of June's parents. This was in early 1989. Bloody long time ago, ain't that the truth. We had only just started our journey together, yet there seem ed to be a certainty about it. Was there some reason for this or is it that a quest is reason in itself?

Well, after the beat down I took at the hands of three guys, the van, the highs and lows, I was running on pilot-light mode. Contact remained with PPE we met in Surfers, as we watched this story unfold. June somehow got me strong again.

No one did anything for the kids in town. June got us working in the community, helping them be heard and reclaiming their streets. We have not stopped since – we listen and guide: 'You wouldn't let a child put a fork in a toaster' (June). That's the mistake made by the people who say, 'Give the kids what they want!' Consult, but you need to guide as well sometimes, don't you? Why are people driven to this sort of life? We've been there, made the mistakes – don't want to lose more lives. When you see so many in the same field for the money; when you see the masses vote in governments who have admitted lying to the people; when you see people more concerned about their time than the other PPE's; it sometimes gets to you and you must find forgiveness inside your being to continue.

June somehow guided stuff in our life, her daughter moved in with us after I ran away for two months to find out that missing component in my life: a mother, who just through being there, would have given me more info on Females! They are the HO and we are the sponge.

Gaining more hope from a few aware people in the public sector, we were able to do some work with an impact on the culture of graffiti. Some would come to trust us, as was necessary if we were to have more insight into this birth of truly international youth art movement. We ain't dogs! We saw young artists in conflict with the system; we didn't see too many who didn't want to be seen. What's it all about? Why do they do it? Can you tell me who this one is? We will work with you if you can keep a list of tags and names. Can you just stay in my electorate? Can you just do a trail in a small space? NO!

In these years of being inside this culture, we have seen again and again some level of government try to answer their communities' concern about this so-called damage to its financial well-being. They usually run programmes that are based on entrapment theories put together by some wannabe superhero type. 'Don't worry, I'll save you.' Get the picture? Or, on the other hand, some bleeding heart with good intentions, who lacks the invention to complete their work. These programmes have in many cases been a part of the learning curve for the modern graffiti writer.

Lesson 1:

Never give your real name or address.

Lesson 2:

Always remember these youth workers, who believe that this is a good place for them to connect with you, work for the Man.

Lesson 3:

While the smokescreen is in place (either while the youth worker is getting pizza or even just looking the other way), *steal as many cans as you can*. As you know from the older, more experienced writers, these suckers knock off at 4 p.m. And they won't dob you in because it would make them look silly, wouldn't it?

Lesson 4:

　　If the cops turn up, leave.

Lesson 5:

　　Never do your usual stuff. Have a legal tag so as not to let others, who you don't know, into your life. **Hip hop ain't all about graffiti.** I gotta learn to spell.

By the way, the X-ray was done this morning. Doctor said no break. I said thank you and left. Looking at the X-ray later and I only need one more to complete the set of a full-sized skelly. Junes and I think they got it wrong again. Still fighting with the mother-in-law who's trying to fight cancer (tough old buzzard – if anyone's gonna beat it, she will). Letting her win is not a thought that could cross my mind at this fork in the roadway. Letting her off lightly is… I sat with her man tonight and was told the story of his working life after I spoke about his current job. I think my shoulder is broken just in the right spot.

Hip hop is an international subculture with art at it's core. Rapping is one of hip hop's most dollar-driven components $$
$$

Westsideast $
My bling (ref your local teenager)
Break-dance: the dance of the streets.

We were only beginning to scratch the surface. DJs were in international competitions. Back in 1989, June and I were flavour (that's flavour, Art) of the month for one year. We lost count of how many print media stories we invoked, with our gallery openings, exhibitions, national awards, social comment, and my favourite was a phone call to a Brisbane radio station. They ended up changing the time in Queensland and having a hand in the downfall of a government that believed that the buck stopped somewhere else other than in their hands. What a high!

　We worked all night to pay the bills as the galleries made little, if any, profit. I was asked to set up a celebration on the beach for daylight saving. I had been given a trial period. After no sleep and a glass or two of champagne, there I was, live across Australia, on *Good Morning Australia*. Mike Gibson spoke to me through an earpiece from Sydney. He asked me why I thought the government had changed its mind. I replied that they had just had an 'ekka' up here (that's the shortened, slang word for 'exhibition') and the greatest bovine ever to grace a ring had been entered in the show. It was from south of the border, in a town called Uki (*you-kie*), so this had the farmers jealous as it was from a zone that had brought in daylight saving many years ago. Laughter was heard and the chicken leg was finished off during this fifteen minutes of fame. (U were wrong Andy, it was never as you see it to be).

I gave June a kiss goodnight/morning and walked along the beachfront towards our rented unit that had the best views of the whole Gold Coast from the top of Rainbow Bay/Snapper Rocks. June went on her way to keep the dayshift happening in the gallery and paint her characters. It pulled people in watching her spray paint as I left the beach to enter Boundary Street. I noticed that that place of worship for many, the pub, was just opening so, as this was my evening, having worked through the darkness, I decided to share my joy of having just changed the time in QLD.

There was one old man, one barmaid and I. I was bursting to feel the accolades of the world as this superhuman feat could only have been performed by one who had been chosen by mighty powerful gods. My world had been turned inside out and upside down. The freshness was oozing from this pumped young prince of the poor.

Fading curtains wha, wha,
Fading curtains wha, wha
(the osmonds' crazy horses)

'How you going, mate?' I asked the bloke at the bar, desperate to share my perceived greatness.

'Got a smoke?' was the drawn reply. 'So what?' was the answer to my next attempt.

Woke up later that day and went back to the graveyard shift at a local estate behind the football club I played for when I was even younger. The fence between this estate and club is the state border of New South Wales and Queensland. I was sacked from that job for keeping myself warm on a cold night and breaching dress code: one coolknight! This was maybe two of the reasons for the move to June's home town. My picture still hangs in that footy club, and I'm proud of that. June has her memories of that club in not such a positive way. This space is for her:

Even though the galleries were no breadwinners we kept them going for over ten years, based in June's home town where I sit here typing this now. Sometime during this night work time June's friend had been to visit with her new man's daughter. We had the pleasure of meeting this bloke earlier that year at a casino where we had been invited to dinner. June's friend is younger than her yet somehow had attached herself to this shady fart who was old enough to be her dad. Upon arrival at the casino we had to wait for the slime to sleaze some dinner tickets from the high-roller room. Not sure, but methinks this is achieved by pretending to be someone you are not. June's sis had brought along a girlfriend, so when slime appeared from the HR room with the magic tickets he was one short. June and I had little money at this moment (for much of our time together we have shared another kind of wealth). Yet after the high roller had 'fessed up to being a little short on the dollar front, we decided to cover the shortfall and in we all went and sat down. Four free meals, 1 2 pay 4. Sleaze ordered the seafood, so did I. Staff who knew of slimy due to his previous use of this scam for food, placed finger bowls on the table, as is the custom in such places. Sleazebag explains to me that this water in the soup bowl is called a **finger bowl**. I pick up the garnished water in my hands and, leaning forward, the bowl finally meets my lips. My head is flung backwards as the cold liquid slides down my throat. Placing the bowl carefully on the table I proclaim, 'Could do with some more lemon!'

You have always been a toy, older man, with your need to lie to those who are not there to harm you. Well, you only ever live once and, as we all saw, you have the freedom to be a fuckhead.

Look me in the eye,
Or are you afraid
You might fry, tough guy?
U need
Love-need.
Buy buy, butt.

As a four-year-old I did some finger-painting in kindy, swirling around and up and down. The teacher asked what it was. I explained that it started as a small kitten and now the kitten's lost in this giant ball of wool. Elders v older; not everyone is an elder. Some people just become older.

The media is in trouble for some Islamic cartoons. There is international outrage. Our media can declare war on its own without a whimper from our government. Something ain't right here… Media? I mean, these cartoons have resulted in religious protest throughout the Muslim world yet the war on our own shores is not given its true exposure. Most graffiti writers are in a network, only one needs to read this declaration for all to shoulder arms. Can't we make a law that helps put political correctness to this act of hate? War.

Insert praying mantis cartoon < headless male <wife. You're having an a affair aren't u?

<blockquote>
It's not a crime
2 spit a rhyme
About your time.
We must sing 2 1 another…
I heard the drum
And the words did come…
We must sing 2 1 another
Oldmandad.
That's MR Oldmandad 2 u.
</blockquote>

It's 3.31 a.m. on 10 February 2006 and I gotta story to tell. June's crying and maybe that's because I'm here with an old street rap CD on. That's real.

Bustamoves is playing as some kind of techno remix. Oh, what did the grand master flash? Someone found a new way to sell this same old rhyme. I think I have seen this before. Yes. Pure hip hop on the remix, techno, digital, house, drum and bass, jungle, didjeridoo, etc. etc. Well, the one track I put down on the hip hop side was spoken word; it just had one of my polyrhythm of didge added to it. I had laid this down when we had very little money, and with June's support I had chased an idea I had to its finish. I had laid down three tracks over the top of each other years before with Dan, the sound guy, (**butterflies in a brookfield backyard**). Dan decided to lay this track that he still had under his table somewhere in his studio under this story I told in rhyme, about the life of a writer the way I saw it, as I had seen enough to need to download it before it was blurred.

FOX

Go van go go, go van go go
I was just 13 when I noticed
Friends doing shit that I ain't.
They were chasing balls,
Riding boards, join the scouts.
Shit! All I wanna do is paint
I wanna do real dope burners'
Shit! Where do I go 2 get my learners?
This is jack in a box,
Is this a consumer joke?
What's wit the art? I wanna do ads 4 Twistes, Prima & Coke.

Go van go go, go van go go.
Teacher spies me doing a
Puzzle, in me own book.
'U shouldn't b doing that here!
Now give me a look.'
She didn't say the magic word,
So piss off u halfstepping bitch
U r always down on me,
Can't u find someone 2
Scratch that itch?

A handful of my hair attaches
Itself 2 her fist & off we go.
My puzzle & me,
Off 2 the principal,
My first private show.

Go van go go, go van go go.
'Don't go writing in your
Schoolbook, sonny.
Don't go writing at all.
We want u 2 play football,
Sonny.
We want u 2 kick the ball.
Don't go writing in your
Schoolbook, sonny,
Or you'll b the next 2 fall.'

Go van go go, go van go go.
When I had devised a plan
Well, I had no money,
That's y I racked the can.
Doing my first panel
I was involved in a chase.
Shit! Video surveillance!
Now they got a handle
On my face.
At least I got up.
People should understand.
It changes everyone's life,
'Cause I'm a wanted man.

Go van go go, go van go go
@ the age of 19 I'm dope king
Of my crew.
School of the streets,
I've paid my due.
Dae put it on me, da community
Is paying 4 my guile.
That's wack, what da fuck?
Y don't dae recognize
My style?
3 of me mates r now dead.
Jimmy's mum keeps asking
What the shit was going on
In his head.

Go van go go, go van go go.
My skills r now in da house
With da flow.
With the anger & poise of a
Caged animal,
On with da show.
Busted piece'n as night turned
2 day.
Walls surround me,
All painted grey.

Go van go go, go van go go
Now I'm 23 & on da street again
Haven't done a burner since
I don't know when.

The man calls me an artist
When he wants
A cheap sign done
Look'n 4 a wall 2 xpress
Myself I can't find one.
Street art sign stands
Legal 4 da world 2 c
Wake da fuck up,
There's thousands of kids
Out there, just like me.

Go van go go, go van go go.
Regression, suppression,
Mmmmanic depression.
I cut off me ear,
Send it 2 da government,
It might help them hear.
Blood running inda streets
As I make the mailbox.
Cunning, wiley, sneaky vandal
I wrote fox.
Divided we stand,
United we fall.
And if our backs should ever
B against the wall,
Let's hope there's a piece there
Done by u 4 me…

C P 1996

Proud Dad

Yesterday was uncle PPEs birthday and the day before was my daughter's. After a fighting/family-style start to her special day, she wowed me with her knowledge of w/bitchcraft with some fake tears, poorly disguised, as she was laughing till she nearly wet herself during what could have been an escalating stand-off between dad & nan. This she knows with her eyes closed.

> You've gotta listen 2 this, you've gotta listen
> (repeat < repeat<repeat)
> 4 ever
> (insert techno rhyme)
> Start of the bettering.

Later she had a great day at school (**first day with her cast off her broken right arm that had been on for thirteen days**). She had a birthday cake in class with the teacher and was left with only her fingers to lick as everyone shared in a small slice of being eight. Daughter/Dad proud, as we were walking down the hall on her big day and she was discussing her best gift which was a kiss on the cheek. Then, without drawing breath, she asked, 'Do you know whose birthday it will be tomorrow? (**Uncle Bill's**) Sssssssswwwwwwwwweeeeeeeeettttttttt luvmuch.**

Rang the cops today to ask why they thought two wrongs make a right. You see, they have been running around the home town spraying stencils over tags. And last week they went out on a construction site to spray over some toy tags. No traffic controls were invoked for this. Paint worker po-lice are gods, so I rang to find out why they step out from their blue line to bitch slap toys, upsetting our process in this zone. I was told the death of a PPE was that PPE's own fault, but no one gave this PPE the rope. Also there was a rumour (**RIP, I saw u**) that we were tagging these walls so as to make them a part of your mural process which employs PPEs. What? My door is open, piggy. Stop the huff'n and puff'n. Meeting with his super on Monday to get this wrong right.

Are u ready to battle,
U blue and white cattle?
Gonna make your handcuffs rattle.
(Oink oink oink oink oink all the way home).

It just seemed odd that the northside po-lice give us spray cans they had collected from busted writers to help us paint our community murals, yet in our home town they will not even discuss our experience, just act like jealous rednecks. Judged before the lips moved.

This little piggy went to tag over tags and not think about the consequence of this on the community. There are only two types of PPEs: the good and those on their way to that peaceful place. Please try to get there soon ASAP piggy-PPE. When I rang the cop we were fixing a mural that some toys had tried to piece over at the Surfers Paradise Girl Guides' hall at Bundall. Just picked up the morning paper and, to my surprise, there was a story of a near abduction on the front page. An eleven-year-old girl had screamed 'Fire, fire!' and escaped these low-life dudes, something she had learnt at the Girl Guides. Guides come in all shapes and sizes. My head is heavy with the thought that we really ain't that long out of the trees are we? May these fuckers be unsuccessful in this form of wealth creation and try another before they hurt the innocent. Fuckfuckfuuckfuccckkffuucckkfucckfuckfuckfuckkk.

The spectre of death has sat heavy over our house, with cancer, broken bladders, broken arm, colitis and cataracts in the mix simultaneously walking the floor. No, no, no; don't feel for us, prepare for it, as we all get our turn, as sure as life itself. Look for strength from whatever floats your boat. Enjoy the joys of truth. Lies, lies; someone's annoying my life with lies …so I shut off… Why?… 1988 me.

It's so good to learn stuff, never too young for that. Our daughter knows more at eight than I knew at compulsory voting age. **Sweeeeeeeeeeeettttt**. We must sing to one another.

1989: Daylight savings, newspaper, radio and TV, local and national.
        Friendships made.

1990: Cilly the Bunyip (yes, June was stuck inside the break-dancing bunyip.
        No one can bust a move to 'Can't Touch This' like her, spinnin' on
        a 14 kg head on stage); Kakadu Cal, Edgar the Echidna (June loves
        dressing up), Koala town. Night shift as a security dude; our casino
        dinner with the used car salesman; porn night with your friend
        ('Hold on to your pants dudes, methinks it's gonna blow!'); early
        insights into the community art worker's life: from the new youth

development officers to the first legal brothel. Legals v. illegals, can control. Demands from the man; festivals.

1996: Olympics, Warana, youthfest ×2, the hip hop music/break-dance/DJ promoters (no talent sleaze); the late nights, House of Pain, Coolio interview (June painted the gangsta in paradise). The gangsters/wannabes, the young artist trying to find a way out of this cocoon by da lagoon, the boys and their girls – young souls of our future elders.

Road Trips

Lice may b a cover 4 da book?
Some people have a way of making little
Things look big.
Some people have a way of making big
Things look little.
Same line space.
This is a good thing?
'Hi! My name is Singer!'
'Why do they call you that?'
'Cause I sing the song that helps right the wrong.'

Magpie

Hmm I'm a magpie.
Hmm I'm a magpie.
U know I don't see in
Black & white.
What makes one man wrong
& one man right?
I c confusion in da world 2day.
Who knows da price our
Children will pay.
What of da colour of my skin
Da human race
Is my next of kin.

Hmm I'm a magpie
Hmm I'm a magpie
I don't mind who live next 2 me
I live in da proverbial
Family tree.
So long as my family
Has some space.
The honour of my neighbour
I won't disgrace.
I haven't lost concern
4 da human plight.
Given a choice,
It's 4 da animals I would fight.

Hmm I'm a magpie
Hmm I'm a magpie
Look at da world
Through da animals eye
This we should all do
B4 we die
4 the dreaming they have
Come 2 give.
Da animals of da world
Have a rite 2 live.
Hmm I'm a magpie,
Come on let's sing da song
Da song that helps right
Da wrong.

Hmm I'm a magpie
Hmm I'm a magpie
Look real close,
Look in 2 my eye.
You'll c y I'm called magpie.

K F C 1993

Da Bomb

And what do you do?
The longer the media hides
The truth,
The more we are
Driven to get it right.
Jazzi is loved by her mummy and daddy
And big sister berry much.
Sodearmo fo@mass fear.
Graffiti genocide
As decided by the misguided.
We must sing 2 1 another;
Our goal is to get our plan
2 da man,
So help us if u can.
The answer is simple
When I smile there's a dimple.

The youth in this international subculture have identified the zone they paint. The urban transit network is usually the home of the true graffiti writer. That's right, wherever the train or bus will get to within a greater city region, i.e., Sydney, Penrith, Newcastle, Wollongong, Manly, Palm Beach, Cabramatta, Balmian, Cronulla, Redfern, 1 zone Brisbane, Tweed, Ipswich, Sunshine Coast, Fairfield, Pine Rivers, Wynnum, the valley, Caboolture, Surfers Paradise...

For so long councils have tried to solve the graffiti issues in isolation, which only causes frustration to this alienation worse. Most of the bullshit that's planned out over a desk in some well-meaning fucker's office will or has not been proven to be successful. As the need to on sell successful programmes is one of the factors that give these fuckers an out, we don't want to put them under too much scrutiny. We might find holes in their successes. Many times have we attended graffiti conferences only to be shocked by the need for people representing the people to treat these gigs as a holiday. Even worse than that is the so-called experts having their pants pulled down verbally by our group in front of the people that might have thought they were getting the best practice placed before them, while the establishment allows and rewards those with little or no experience to work in fields they don't know. We will continue to reap what we sow.

On one side the buffers (removalist) talking about the can, use this latest snake oil 2 deal with this problem. You see, we put this grey two-pack on the wall in case someone puts some colour on it. We can remove it with a toxic chemical. These are real people who have or are making a living on the efforts of the graffiti culture. We want to put these guys out of business, legally. With our clubs placed around the region with levels similar to others such as football, bridge, surf, tennis, you get it. Interaction between the clubs in friendly competition is one of the things we need to fully achieve our outcome of bringing these underground PPEs and the wider community together. We will all be better off if this goal can be achieved. June has the know-how to put this in a format that will meet the legal requirements that are a part of achieving this outcome on a global scale. Yes, that's right, I said global.

Now that we have that point cleared up, on to the zones. Stop, please stop your local programmes that don't go anywhere and join together for a positive outcome for all. You cannot think that an area or council border stops these PPEs from entering your space. Sometimes doing nothing at all proactively can be better than teaching young PPEs thinking about the graffiti lifestyle the guidance for some exhilarated skilling up or learning, and then taking the water out of the pool they learnt to swim in. That would be criminal wouldn't it? ('SmartArts' on one side and 'who's da crim?' on the other; that's been on our van – copywrited – since 1996.) Entrapments happen as an outcome for these types of programmes.

Young PPE at home: 'Dad, you know how I want to do graffiti?'

'Yes, son/daughter.'

'Well, they got this legal happening, Dad. Can I go?'

'Yeah, PPE. So long as the council says it's OK I can't see why not.'

PPE develops a hunger for the fame of being a writer. PPE's still a long way from that yet the hunger still burns, the smell of the fumes (look after yourself and your family), the thrill of the risks that must be taken as the funding was never properly in place. The best our organisation can do without the whole of playground approach (zone) supported by far less funding than these collective councils, states, federal governments (the peoples) need to address this concern at this current time. They have their collective heads in the bucket of sand we see as being the same full of shit anyway. The local council decides that it must be able to address such lowbrow crime. The state does not have a hand in such matters unless they are staging a major international event (e.g. the World Expo, the Olympics, the Commonwealth Games, the Beef Fest, etc.) on which they usually spend millions, and plan years in advance. Lots of finger-food with fuckwits' functions are preludes to these types of events. Throw the crusts this way sir, madam.

State and federal come together with funding to remove the graffiti from the walls that have tags, pieces on them. Some of these markings older than the short-term employed whose short-term employment is to buff (i.e. remove). Tabloids run a series of war crime stories on the international subculture with a finger clearly seen rotating in their navel. The blind have more of chance of writing a letter about what they cannot see (**with much respect to those who have visual trouble - I know this handicap doesn't affect your ability to see**).

The po-lice slip a couple of undercovers into this locally divided culture. What does that mean? Well, you see, different crews work the same zone, sometimes crossing paths, sometimes cross-pollinating (**a member from one joins the other, perhaps as subcontractors, maybe because they have been rejected by their own crew. Perhaps this is through a chance meeting at gigs, or the worst case is when the premeditated is involved, which can included violence, paint wars, harassment, home invasions, dumb hate-driven shit and even terror**). Don't dog is the code. Torture is a way of extracting info from young writers with bed-wetting problems, or even two or three minutes in a waiting dock at the local blue room will loosen the tongues of those whom are not lifers. So we have hailed the saviour of the cosmetic. A filter with holes big enough to let through all community ills and corruption while celebrating another bust. The judge must weigh all these ills that had fallen through against the urinating in public charge brought before the court. (**Didn't Andy piss on some copper and sell it to the same masses as art?**). Still ready to battle.

You see now what we know. Its own division is like a survival switch painted on walls in my favourite colour, 'clear'. If someone found a way to paint here, it's a safe bet another will as well, so in time the walls can build up so much paint that it falls off. Start again. Repeat. Repeat. Success. Success. Defeat. Defeat. Beat. Beat. As I knock you off the seat with one of my feet. You went over me when I wasn't complete. Many when financially able won't buy drugs, they buy paint in flavours they then will paint on a surface knowing that it might not even be on that surface for twenty-four hours. This is an insane and extreme art game or just plain insane which can be used in the computer-monitored court rooms of our lives as a defence for one's actions (as Roms is dragged from a wall in close to his cribb by two po-lice officers whilst still spraying with a can in each hand). Word, Romsie. He's a round peg looking at thousands of square holes. He has shown over the twelve years that we have known him that he will find a way to get a public canvas. He walks through the sands of time, without sinking, being looked upon as somewhat of an enigma. Yet he has a child he hasn't been able spend time with. This will play out as this child who must be five or six by now starts the calling that happens without cost. (Much respect you crazy mo_fo hip hop PPE, for you could see long ago. June & Cal. Thanks dude).

What, a writer with no crew? How did that happen? Well, you see, eagles don't flock (Billy) the supply and demand department is still looking into it. What did this dude see? I hope it was something that's real and he believes there is hope on the planet that is our home. It's a strange time when we have to send PPEs from our zone to another to fight for a belief that is shared with our trading partners. Yet this is against our trading partners. So as to not slip out of bed with our warmonger Christian-backed buds may we always cook our peas different ways as we will surely die if we try to air condition the planet. 21°C, three litres of H2O, 37.4 g of food blend and a treadmill: fuck! What more could anyone desire? Only one boss in charge of a human shit factory! And don't fuck the system or your DNA will, (really has to be removed or deleted from programme). Cease!

koala dreaming

There's a baby bird on a
Branch just above me.
It's waiting 4 its feathers
So it can b truly free.
If he leaves the nest 2 early
He will surely die.
He should wait 4 his feathers
B4 he gives it a try.

Yeah, that's right, I'm a koala.
I sleep 19 hours a day.
All that dreaming gives
Me a right 2 say:
Don't run 2 fast or you'll
Stub your toe.
We've only got one world
There ain't nowhere else 2 go.

As a human child will
Crawl then walk.
Your human leaders must
Listen, then talk.
Don't run 2 fast or
You'll stub your toe.
We've only got one world
There ain't nowhere else to go.

The human pollution has
Reached critical mass.
There are humans employed
2 make toxic gas.
It's like dare's no global limit
No limit 2 greed.
Stop stuffing up da planet
Who planted da human seed
Don't run 2 fast or you'll
Stub your toe
We've only got one world
There ain't nowhere else 2 go.

As the wind blows pollutants
& poisons around.
Even if u don't know what
You're look'n 4, u must know
What u have found.
Your industrial revolution
Has provided pollution
4 da sake of all our children
I demand a solution.
Don't run 2 fast or you'll
Stub your toe.

We have only got one world
Dare ain't nowhere else 2 go.
In the last 200 years there has
Been a major change.
Don't go look'n at me!

You're the one dats strange.
I'm not saying everything
You've done is wrong
Because only a superior being
Could invent a plastic thong.
Don't run 2 fast or you'll stub
Your toe.

KFC 1994

If you listen to the chorus
And yell 'don't run!' then
Mumble '2 fast or you'll stub
Your toe,' u will know
What it is to be
Walking the dog with me.
Ccc
Need 2 straighten the knee
Walk out 2 the dunny
& have a pee-pee.
It's all right folks, remain
Seated, everything came out OK.
Art is the thing we started
Doing after f.e.s
(Fucking, eating, sleeping)
It may b the root of all evil as
We all know that worth of
Our money is designed into it.
'Survival is the consequence
Of creativity' – me, 2005.
Some say this way,
Some say that,
Yet it must b said the fat cat
Is lazy.

So it should be said that
The industrial revolution
Has turned us crazy.
U can earn enough 2 become
Hazy.
Suck in this consumer shit and
Go forget 2 pick the daisy
Printed the above.
-==-=0=00=-0=9-9=-=-09-
=0=99=98=-9=88-8089=09=80-8594-
JPEAO8302=420==12
Crack the code.
Advertising at the youth and hip hop
Lolly pop at the bus stop,
That advertises the car with
The poptop,
And the latest designer
Fashion mop.
Stop, stop, stop. (This is where we place fridge magnets)
Sometimes I wonder why the
media even tries, as they know
what sells.
The kids are our future.
Another miracle.
Happy in the knowledge you
have and accept all
knowledge, process, conclude,
most importantly, don't
Believe the tabloid media.
For they don't want to seek more
knowledge or challenge it.

It rocks

It
U carnt find it
U carnt grind it
U carnt bind it
U carnt, u carnt, u carnt rrrrr re ree rewind it,
U carnt lose it,
U carnt chose it
U carnt refuse it,
U carnt defuse it,
U carnt be it,
U carnt see it.

U carnt knee it
U carnt free it
U carnt snag it
U carnt fag it
U carnt tag it
U carnt bag it
U carnt stick it
U carnt prick it.
U carnt kick it
U carnt lick it
U carnt blow it
U carnt stow it.

U carnt throw it
U carnt flow it
Cause it's nothing.

                                    I-_-I
                                     lll
                                    Cno1
                                    @2006

It rocked a little when the media wanted to sell out on fear. Sydney first, Melbourne Commonwealth Games second, us third. For some it was 'Oh no, here we go again!' For some it was a lot more. Watching kids die is not what I had a plan for in life. So I gave effort to something I love: bringing the media into this space fucker's paradise. The internet is pay TV. A talking library with porn and graffiti everywhere so there is more evidence. The DVD 'How to do it' guide is a pisser. Even inside the TV set in every living room of Casey in Vic. Is the stuff they have got on the outside where their children play? Wonder how the hip hop sellers take it to the masses in Casey; got your own TV station selling Casey, independently without the advertising dollars of the corporates. You stop hip hop? Ha! Join us in giving the youth a lesson and stop feeding them to desert antz. Graffiti can be used to educate them when this happens.

Learn it before
We next meet on a seat
Ready made 4 defeat
Cause I got more answers
Than Pistol Pete.

Our status in the costume character world didn't come with a monetary reward. And even making it to the awards we needed support through local fundraising and bartered deals. So there was a character invented called Kakadu Cal who was Cilly the Bunyip's (mythical swamp/billabong creature – June's of course) straight guy. This was one time me bitch, who had *oscolee-i-tis* (sic) – a bent spine from the polio she had contracted at seven years old from the vaccine dose at school – showed a huge amount of strength. In a mad move by June, she let me make magic, dudes.

That reminds me: yesterday, 10 February 2006, I took nine kids aged near eight to see a shit flick, 'Bigmumma 2', that seemed to be too long for the kids at 100 minutes. Worse than that, the character Desert-Ant didn't work for me. He was carrying this 14 kg costume head around for four comedy/break-dance shows a day, as if to say 'Fuck the pain!' Pain, art: something we learn from almost every day. The title for Cilly and mates was 'The Environ-mental Crusaders'. The kids were really good after entering the complex (didn't that word mean difficult sometime in recent times?) in a loud congo line. This was received with the smiles of all inside, showing that a good thing is just that.

'Water, thanks, x 3.'

'That's $12.75 please, sir.'

'Fuck.'

But the kids need to be kept so I accept this trade. Ponder the cost of fridge magnets. In the last couple of days there have been multiple attempts at stealing kids off the side of streets in south-east Queensland. My fear on this day was that our society, which sometimes looks without seeing, is not reaching into the fire while another is burning. As we exited the theatre into the complex, nine eight-year-olds ran to the front like eight-year-olds do in an air-conditioned paddock. I hoped I was not going to find the mayor of Woolygong there, waiting to steal what he never needed in the first place. It's all good, now. Still, we have this as something that the media has not declared war on. Fuck fuck fuck wit wit wits.

Thursday 9 February 2006

Playing Mr Squiggle over some bombing that some toys had done on a Girl Guide hall and baseball dug-outs in this park in Bundall, Gold Coast. This is not what most writers do; they usually have respect for others.

> Will c u l8r toys,
> Don't b scared as we
> Are yet 2 have a fist fight
> Over this sort of thing.

But we do love and that can be scary to some who are yet to experience this. Anyway, still takin' medication and needing to address the issue of the home town po-lice who are painting stencils over tags. Must play cowboy on the highway. A phone call to find out why:

'Yes, sir, he will return your call when he gets back from court.'

Ring a ding a ding.

'Yes. Calvin speaking (singing) about this really cool thing we got happenin'. For we have the support of some (love out to you all).'

Po-lice man tells of his power and doesn't want to see what I see. He got a little fired up and said that he had heard rumours (**RIP**) that our group were tagging these walls. To which I reply that our door is open and that he is welcome to be with me over a cup of tea so as to see what we can see. I wished that I had told him of the rumour (**RIP**) of his small penis. Oh, right. It didn't start until the end of that empowering call.

I rang the number I already had stored in my phone to connect with Kelly in the super's office. Kelly said that he was a busy man and I could see him within three weeks, to which I replied that I would be seeing the minister before that.

'And what time on Monday would you like to see him?' was her response. Can't wait to see if he can see what we see. Will update this soon as.

13 February 2006

Meanwhile, back at the cookie jar, my daughter brought some fortune cookies. Mine read, 'A conclusion is simply the place where you got tired of thinking.' June's read, 'A scholar's ink lasts longer than a martyr's blood.' Jazzi's, 'You can't expect both ends of the sugarcane to be sweet.' Something in that for all methinks.

Had a vivid dream yesterday avo. This house was empty and a recycling truck was reversing down a grass slope with me sliding behind it, pondering my next move if I was to have one, when my phone rang and woke me. Full colour, with the beeping sound of the reversing truck, the word that rhymes with 'luck' and 'fuck'. I am trying to see what the reason for this dream was. Its object was to make me remember to include the 'Environ-mental Crusaders' (**thanx PC**).

The conclusion you may be reading this book for is simple. Art clubs, in association with each other, will eventually provide graffiti writers with an area for use. Saving money in cleaning costs will be one of the reasons that this will happen. It is so simple to look back sixty years to the surf culture which was not an illegal yet still underground (or underwater) bunch of hippies with salt in their veins. No one wanted their daughters to go out with a semi-nudist riding around in the ocean all day and God only knows what sort of sacrifices were made at night to Huey the wave god. Now look at the underground above. Surf has many benefits in our community: various levels of competition for both young and old in numerous disciplines, with childcare on the beach while mum and dad compete in the water. The economic benefits of this culture are what must be considered as a new workplace as it is. It is the same with the art clubs addressing the desire which our youth have expressed for thirty plus years now.

Did you know that surf culture artwork is done by artists who started their art lives in graffiti and are still involved in this culture? Yes, there are mentors in place for when the funding comes to help the youth become as accepted as those hippie surfie scum have. Not everyone who buys a surf product surfs, or is likely to become a world tour pro (**waskally wabbit**). So it will be with competition in the art clubs.

Participation is the key (**over to you, dear, as I know you have already written a club system that the man can understand**). It has to be said that while the media isn't interested in debate on this subject, our whole way of life is being fucked over by these sell-kings keeping the population @mass fear. So many are into the profit that they want to suppress the views that we put forward as if we are some kind of false prophets. The need to continue is strong as we have done no wrong.

Graffiti will be an educational tool, as it has to be. We're going back again to 1989 (June, I need some help here, dear, to make it all clear). Everyone cooks their peas differently. Much of the stuff we have learnt along the journey will never bring back those who passed away at the beginning of their lives. Thinking of you now. Sorry we couldn't put the fingers on the keys earlier. It's like we were still growing ourselves and your lives where never in conflict with ours. Much respect.

1993-1994

With June's ability to write grant applications, pity she doesn't get time to paint as she is the talent the boys aspire to be like. For worthwhile projects we were on the field and ready to play: the first little steps to destiny. A little funding started the ball rolling towards many discoveries. One of these was that supply would be falling well behind demand. Another was that, despite the lack of space for writing, some in the culture would not enter the legal place due to the fact that previous programmes had been based on entrapment. Other factors that caused concern were personal exclusions due to crew loyalties and an inability to produce what had been bragged about. During the previous two to three years, a TV crew had done an undercover story following a local crew on a bombing raid and into the train yards, piecing [painting] trains. The TV station were forced by law to hand over the video to po-lice. In and around that time the crew battles turned nasty, with bricks in the face during home invasions. There was a CMS crew – 'crush more skulls'. Strange that, as time goes by, only a few people would know who these guys were. And why would one of this crew remember me? Early this year, 2006, thirteen years on, this guy doing rehab says, 'I remember you from the BMX club legal and Warana!' (**I'll come to that soon**). He was in CMS and asked if I knew that Loti, the dual international in rugby, was in CMS too. I explained some of our journey and goals, and we compared **RIP** lists. He expressed an interest to be involved in the club system if it is to get up and running as he felt addicted to graffiti. And ponder a different outcome to his life if they had been running when we first met.

> From talented young artist
> 2 kids lucky not 2 spray
> Themselves in the face.
> This is where practice was trying
> 2 take place.
> Hand me another can of mace,
> While I retie my shoelace,
> Fuck off the 2 of u, get that
> Camera & brick off me face.

Ain't it amazing grace?
Booran park & the BMX club r
Painted over, recycle this space.
Old sckool gone without trace.
Add a little drum & bass. Stace.
2 say at a political level it was
Da blind leading da blind would
B very unkind.
These motherfuckers had their
Eyes closed and both hands out
& dats still the case.
Funding drying up, all da
Do gooders gone, left
Without a legal place.
June puts 2gether a concept of
Youth having a say.
The Brisbane Warana festival
Will soon b underway.
Off 2 da botanical garden
4 xpression, (hip hop needs 2 harden
2 high school), 2 c what we could,
Look'n 4 youth insight
Hope'n it's all good.
We workshop some battle rhymes
That could shout out of da times.

I remember one outcome: walking Brisbane with some Year 11 girls from a church-based school screaming,

Chirac, he is really stupid
He blew up a nuke head
Underneath da c.
Chirac, he is just a retard,
Should do it in his backyard,
Where only he can ccc…

over and over, louder and louder; then having this performed on the '100% in control' Queensland Health Youth Stage that we had arranged. There were also rappers, DJs, break-dancers and writers, some of whom were paid to be there due to June's ability as an artist to create. Over nine days continuously, eight of them paint a 12 ft by 8 ft canvas. There was no bombing in the gardens, no violence, no crews battling with anything but their skills; but, most importantly, no money worries, as after paying all the hip hoppers there was fuck all left.

Nine days in the city's main park with the unity in the hip hop community (which was for the public and press perceptions, anyway) and for all the months of work that went into this, the financial reward felt like something had been stolen, a real fucking theft. Well, lookin' back, it seems that way, money-wise. Yet at the time we didn't give a fuck, 'cos this has never been about the money, sonny, runny Easter bunny. We had a climax day with polys receiving message sticks from the youth. And I wasn't hiding – yeah, that was me with bandages all over my face on the roof. Word up, ask the missus, that's the truth. At the time the mayor of Brisbane whose name was Tim, (**a lad from south weed as his saviour did bleed**), was late for the bus to promote this gig. We were to travel past the buildings and down to the park with the Moreton Bay fig.

> When he arrived on the bus
> There was little time to discuss,
> So I said, 'Tim, surely you could
> Have made it sooner,
> I could have had a schooner.
> His brother I was 2 meet
> On another street.
> His name was bully,
> A smart man he wasn't silly.
> 2 me he once said, 'Eagles don't flock.'
> Y is your brother such a cock?
> How many years a reformed alco
> 2 the Kingscliff Hotel early this year
> With a beer.
> Fuck 'em bully. I still hear.
> Fuzz makes things unclear.
> Clarity is 4 charity in a $ driven
> World yet u still have seen
> The real human bean.
> I know so

I write this flow.
Bro Kombi in tow.
Look 4 a book *The Last Warrior,*
Then u also will know.
Write the show in much the same
Way I'm sitting here reflecting now.

Freestyle. It was a little above the none-schooled kids, yet still visually there for them. The bunyip would only talk to me.

1995

We have now another year
To try and make things clear.
June decides 2 get in2 main
Roads ear.
The same mob her father
Worked with 4 many a year.
They started 2 build walls 2
Stop the sound
Where graffiti might b found.
With wisdom of some old boys
We start about the bringing
2gether of the toys
(oh well it rhymes).
Everyone has 2 start
Somewhere and on the train
Lines it's not as easy as it was
Back in da day.
These new canvases were
Prime targets 4 what the
Young writers had 2 say.
It's that level of concern
That u cannot learn
It's in u or it's not.
Try'n hard not 2 lose the plot.

Da what, I forgot! Not!
Well at one time they got
A drot
2 dig out dirt & make a drain
So as 2 have da water go back
2 the ocean again.
A safe place 4 writers 2 paint
Under da road.
So the graffiti did explode.
In da land of da cane toad.
Public complaining
Graffiti is eye straining.
Then in came Cal & June,
Years singing da hip hop tune.
Funding followed real soon.
With presto in tow,
We were ready 2 blow.
The Waxmaster Wayne show.
Writers from all over came.
Little conflict, what a shame.
Mayb it was the heat 2 blame.
Writers battling with skills.
Not enough $ 2 pay the bills,
What da fuck, here 4 da thrills
Lucky we live rent-free.
Under da mango tree.
2 3 or knot 2 3?
What was the ? – da mark.

This zone
Proved 2 b prone
2 b overthrown.
2 many had claim it their own
A seed had already been sown
43c grown, grown, blown.
Don't give up, back 2 the phone
Moan moan moan.
We still have stay ups there
'Cause we did dare 2 bring a chair
Or was it trestles & a ladder?
Doesn't really matter
This rhyme is getting fatter
U might have yours in crumbs
I'll have mine in batter.
Day after da legal went down
It was time 2 drown.
A storm came by
Dropped a cloud from the sky
Water so deep, up 2 my thigh.
Bye bye.
We must swim 2 1 another!
Treat me like a brother,
'Cos I'm not your lover.
I save that 4 another. June.

1996

7 yrs passed since da tour began.
We new we had a plan
Must b someway 2 get it 2 da man
National graff speak in Perth
I'm there, 4 all dat it was worth.
Bunch of suits talk'n their way
In2 each others' financial pockets.
This was b4 G.S.T. What did they do
With the dockets?
Sat at the back of hall,
All the suits on the stage,
Felt like a village people gig.
Buffo the graffiti slayer d-rage.
When? – da mark time came around,
I made my call
From the back of the hall,
This ain't no time 2 stall,
One might fall.
Yo what's with re-active shit,
Putt'n grey 2pac on concrete?
In case anyone puts colour there
U can remove it with a toxic
Chemical. The snake oil sales
Dudes would all look at me with
Eyes that said, u could b the end

Of me scam
And I am.
Let's take our idea 2 Uncle Sam,
Y don't u peoples at this
National gig look both ways?
Or is it the suntan on the back
Of your rednecks,
Is where it's gonna stay?
Looking at the light,
Might give u a fright.
Turn around, u might
Sleep better at night.
Don't think that 10 years on
U have won your fight.
I'm so fucking right
As u continue the blight
Covering over the graffiti done
In poor light.
From sunset 2 dawn
U make me wanna yawn,
U have the ears of a prawn.
U got nothing 2 help the unborn.
From the pages of history
U will b torn
So go and make yourself useful
And mow the lawn.
2 the writers & b-boys of W.A.
Thanks 4 the hospitality on me
Short stay. I remember it fondly
2 this day. Old valiants, painted

Denim jackets,
Huge international legals,
Rustos, buffers being charged 4
Killing art, legal warehouse,
Chrome rhinos,
Basement breaking in shelltoes.
All in 2 days. Thanks 2 the hip hop
Community extreme westside
With nothing 2 hide
Plenty of pride,
Enjoy the ride,
I'm on your side,
I got your back,
Plenty at that gig who lied.
What about dizzy Lizzy
Da redhead from Brizzy
Who's always bizzy?

She hooked up the big play of the year, fund-raising for the Olympics, paintin'
4 ft by 4 ft boards with young writers so as to sell them to raise money for our
athletes to go to Atlanta USA for the 1996 Olympic Games. We even trialled the
new water-based spray paint on the market, only to find it came out a bit like
shaving cream.

Oh what a dream
Looking 2 install confidence in
These kids 2 young 2 shave.
Beans being beans, these kids did the
Best they could

With shaving cream & small bits
Of wood.
June was sharing her art skills
And finding ways 2 pay the bills.

She also arranged shopping
Centres 2 promote this strange
Show of support 2 our Olympic
Athletes. Remember the launch
At Capalaba; all the boards on
Display 4 the first time.
Hope I remember 2 rhyme.
We display 4 sale over 50 boards
Painted by young writers.
Hip hop stood up on da day,
DJ Sneak, 2 decks, records 2 play
Devise, wink, spit raps 2 'ava spray,
B-boy's busk & versastyles break.
Never forget busk's headspin.
It was him who was drilling for the
Carpark a floor below.
What an amazing hip hop show
Standing next 2 a boxer & the
Olympic head.
'Which one of these should be an
Olympic sport? Him'
(Pointing 2 busk
Doing a headspin)
'Or da bloke next 2 u whose
Sport is trying 2

Knock some1's head off?'
Is what I said.
Dred head feed lead dead.
Donating their skills
2 pay the Olympic bills.
Think back – that just kills.
Or is it that we were dills.
I called it Robin Hood on a
Designer drug.
Well, it felt like we were takin'
From the rich
2 give 2 the rich
In a cultural stitch.
Yet it was really some sharing
Caring & fucking daring
Grey muscle we needed 2 flex.
The opening of this exhibition was
Attended by the mayor, Olympic
Heads & Olympians where da $s went.
Open day and money was spent
We would have been fucked if we
Had 2 pay da rent.
First board was sold 2 the mayor
Painted character by a young
Writer who sold 2 on dat
Day. Touché.
4 the record we raised over $2,400
4 the Aussie team
What a fucking strange dream.
Oh yeah, life's peaches & cream.

If u want 2, now u can scream,
June don't like sport dat much,
Yet she found a way 2 bring 2
Communities 2gether with her
Magic touch.
Federal election in 1996
Let 10 years go
& try 2 stay when u r low.
We received a savage blow.
Announcements were made,
Our plan found shade
Safer Australia grants 2 prove
That we were in d groove
June had done d job
Writing stuff 2 Paul or Bob
Michael Lavarch
Ironed it with starch
The smart art club's underway
With Ruth, Cracknel & Triple J.
Still a price we had 2 pay,
The election went d other way
This effort should b honoured
Then we knew
The struggle was not true blue;
Time 2 stand in d queue.
The incoming knew
What they wanted 2 do.
Fuck, what's with d word
We heard?

It smells like it,
It taste like it,
It turned into a turd,
Just like Saddam with a Kurd
We got gassed.
Time 2 start again,
2 find a new friend
10 years on the bend
This is no way d fucking end
Our lives r here to serve
Not sit on a fuckin' curve.
Stand up if u can
Stand up if u have a plan
4 d man wit d can in da hand
Or shut d fuck up cause we listen.
U 'ave got 2 listen
U 'ave got 2 listen 2 dis
Repeat (4ever)
There might b sumtin u might miss
Cum a little closer
& I'll give u a kiss.
June, can u take over
While I 'ave a piss?
U got 2 listen 2 this.
With all d talk of sedation
U'll find we're on a mission
2 make your nation a better place
No water cannons & mace
4 history 2 trace
So what if this book's in ur face

Workin' with diggers last year
Made it all so clear
Celebrate freedom, 'ave a beer
D Kokoda challenge,
Mudgeeraba 2 Nerang,
96 k, teams of 4, sang
Pay'n the way 4 schoolkids
2 c what our troops did
Freedom fightin' on d skids
4 they had rifles & tin lids.
We supported what felt right
Filming all through d night
As Aussies we r true blue
Glad d many lost 2 d few
Thanx Doug, u knew true blue.
Bin me up if that's what u 'ave 2 do
D Brisbane line
D political wine
Our troops did shine
Is this your country –
Well, I know it's mine.
Respect 4 d effect
Dat saved our neck
Like u were living in heck,
All hands on d deck
We r not a shipwreck
Thanx 2 all who have served.
4 it's they who give us a chance
2 pull down pants
& make a stance.

When u r not listenin'
The prison bell is ring'n.
Shall I stop sing'n?
Fuck u, I'm Australian,
And fuckin' proud.
How else would I b allowed
2 b next 2 d governor general
4 our member of parliament 2 c
Me b'n me? Said, 'Suppose dat takes
Us of d terrorist list?'
I wasn't even pissed
Next saw her at her secretary's
Daughter's engagement party
That almost rhymes with her
Last name.
She played our game
Found that she was not lame
Look'n after stand'n on a bindi
She could have been Miss Indy
Hopefully soon, 1 off 2 kindy
D blue card closed d doors
2 them paedophiles maws
8 kids close 2 d Logan River.
Dave, u really did deliver, look
In d book
U'll c a reference 2 B's.
I'm my own man, not on me knees,
Don't hand me d keys
Don't even say please
4 when I find d time

Your film idea would be fine
I'd prefer 2 show d b keeper
B4 d grim reaper.

Mum & Dad, relations went bad
They gave it all dae had.
How is your lad?
We all know of sad
So love is what makes us glad
& that what is in this book.
Take d time 2 take a look.
Read it when u cook.
U might find what's crook,
Or is it that we mistook?
Stand up when u need 2
The diggers had 2

Cno1

P.S. Bartender, a Dr Pepper
4 d ½ stepper.

So dat's what I'm doing, eating life.
Did u c d discount on d fish?
D u ever have a wish
How do red tis ward. Spellcheck.
My favourite colour is clear,
Dat's d way I like it in me ear,
Pool comp's near
Time 4 beer, dear.

1997

Freedom of expression,
The street art exhibition:
Local council gallery
From where sum1 earns a salary.
8 ft by 8 ft canvas 2 put graff on show
War cry, LKR & raceless d flow
B'boy's breakin' was all da go
Tattoo/airbrush artist, Little Mic
Writers and June's art twas sick
So many from heaps of crews
This shit did make the news.
Galleries: no.1 4 views,
Polly's concern was 4 rap dance'n,
Could have given her a pantsen
Maybe listened 2 2 much Hanson.
The mayor with flair,
Who ain't no longer there,
Did show some care
1 of the best air artists in town,
Arrived without a crown
In a pimped-up cut hot ride
He came inside
With nothing 2 hide
Patch on his back he wore, pride.

The mayor nearly shit
He looked like he'd been hit
2 represent art 2day
There's a price u gotta pay.
A church had provided sum pews
So as 4 us 2 create some news
Paint'n in d sun
What a lot of fun
Out of a youth worker's car
Jumps Hexas, u were a star.
'Hey man, can I do a piece?'
'Sorry man, it's like part of d lease.
Come back 2morrow.'
Time we have 2 borrow
It leaves us with much sorrow
As that night u ended dead
With a rope around your head
Almost enough said.
Drank 2 much, wet d bed, Fred.
D day of the goodbye
Many did cry,
That is not a lie
4 he had a good heart
This lateral kid was smart.
D newspooper had
Made dis kid mad
By exploiting all he had
Cause his mother was on harry.
This kid they had 2 bury

Did God have 2 marry
2 give us Jesus our lord?
Dis kid died on his own sword.
Yew sinned. Dis is your reward
U fucking fraud
And I ain't talking 2 d Lord.
$$$$$$$$$$$$$$$$$$$$$$$$$$$$man
Look me in d i if u can
The day of d kids final silent say
We stood toe 2 toe Mr Pay
So I know what's pay day gay way,
4 it's d shit I gotta spray.
Then the magic happened in June,
I was gonna b a father real soon,
We were paint'n d Kingston wall
When I heard d call.
4 one life we created
Now life had been fated
(Dis ain't overstated)
4 we had mated
Only months before.
Do I look 4 d door?
No, life's become so much more.
No, we're bringin' crews 2gether,
Well, ain't we clever?
Some say, it would b never.
Smack d pussies with a feather
All night try'n 2 make d budget right.
Prickhead at the end of d dead-
End street. Kinda give us a fright.

Due 2 his lack of sight
Or confusion wit d light
By saying I give him a fright
I told d man
Dat we had a plan
2 take a can
Dat would make an icon on d land
On a dead-end street.
He would not have 2 compete.
And we did.
As da wall was in the phone book
The next year,
The message was clear.
Only copycats 2 fear
Have we got your ear?
4 the end 2 another life is near.
With PPE's painting 2 d max
Some used drugs 2 relax,
Well, dat's d fax, Max.
How do we defend dis wit tax?
3 levels of pieces d stax
Win international recognition
In d graffiti virate competition.
Young local wanted a position
So high in the middle stay up
We held it as it was his cup.
His brother put up rumour,
Just for some humour.
He tried but never made it back –
Maybe sumtin 2 do wit smack –
So we stuck up the Aboriginal flag.

Was only months l8tr a body bag
4 a parent. 2 lose a son,
This was not fun
Your brother was 2 cop out later.
Fucckkk!
This ain't my cuppa t
And u can stick your biscuit.
If I c a problem I'm a gonna fix it.
I'm skating on thin ice,
Trying 2 survive;
Gotta do this shit, while I'm alive.
If d ice was thicker it wouldn't crack.
I've gotta get these mother-
Fuckers off my back.
The youthfest around dat time
Gave the hip hop crews
A chance 2 change some views.
Writers doing signs made d news
Headline acts & hip hop stage,
MCs doing laps, a lion in a cage.
B'boy's and b'girls hit d floor
2 open d eyes 4 d 1 behind d door
DJs on the 1s & 2s play d score
Off 2 d big day out, hip hop shed
When did we find room 2 bed?
Prove'n 2 unite
D 1's sworn 2 fight
Unreal, grouse, groovy, fly,
Hot, like out of sight dynamite.
Moments in time,

When it all seemed 2 rhyme,
From glam lights 2 crime
Postage stamps by Shime
Exit & seize spin on dime
Match'n plum purple & lime
It's not a crime 2 rhyme
About your time.
We must sing 2 1 another,
Treat me like a brother.
Twas a hot summer night
When I heard those magic words.
'Fuck me. Waters' just broken.'
Off down toll road wit a token,
Hardly a word was spoken,
Lots of coffee & smoking,
The consequence of poking.
1 a.m. to 5.07 p.m: 16 hour labour – u r joking!
While Mummy
Still had bubs in da tummy,
She wrote applications 4 money.
Work 4 d dole. 'You're crazy, honey!'
Our girl was 1 month & 1 day old
When this chapter began 2 unfold.
A path laid with gold
Coming in from d cold
Our actions r of d kind, bold.
Ideas needed 2 be sold.
Someone broke d mold.
The largest mural group on the
Planet, sum1 was told.

Hip hop wasn't put on hold.
Writers employed, artwork sold.
We have murals in over 100 towns,
Jealousy abounds,
D half-stepp'n fucking clowns.
U don't create it wearing frowns.
Rain comes; swim, or sum1 drowns.
The world don't c those sounds.
40 + programmes in 2 & ½years
Nay sayers, graffiti slayers,
Pedaphiles in 2 man's ear.
The message was clear,
They were in fear;
No more work 4 d dole 2 b had.
That made the missus mad
And not that sad,
Might even be glad.
I don't mean wrapped in plastic,
Their words were elastic;
We still had programmes 2 complete,
Hit a feather, still on our feet,
Return 2 the street
While u take a seat
Strange sort of cheat, defeat.
Bring'n writers 2 d community
Proved beauty & unity
With murals 4 all 2 c.
Runs on the board
Still hold'n the sword
Main roads saw value 2 reward

We had good news 4 the board
Thank the Lord.
A saving grace not untoward
At d RSL North Ipswich, the
Announcement was made.
Phantast was 2 paint murals 4
Main roads, extension 2 b paid.
The foundations had been laid,
2 years' murals, no grants
Near tore a hole in d pants.
After the Australia Day Award '99
Came the 2000 Olympic torch
Relay to provide the shine.
D schools did designs 4 d run
That were painted with
Spray cans over the council.
Colours on the power poles
Dry'n power provide by d sun
1,500 poles, 15 towns, two states,
A bombing raid legally done;
Kids got amp certificates, fun,
Provided by the vision, my no.1.
Methinks she's try'n 2 kill me
With her mind that only 1 can c.
Sometime she dreams of the
Forest – I'm only 1 tree.
As we continue 2 grow
Methinks u need 2 know
That we believe art clubs r d go,
It will save u doe,

Just may save an innocent a blow.
There r some who say they know
Like d psyche
At the last national graffiti
Conference in Brizzy, he stand'n b4 a
Crowded/empty hall, explains his
Experience of the day before and
How his camera had searched
Out his reference 2 his speech 4 d
Day. Look at this, what must be
Going through the mind of this
Teenager? Clearly u can c d
Word 'No' written 20 times or more
From the back of d hall,
With no need 4 a mic?
Told this freak 2 get on his bike
'It was sumtin u said I don't like
U make me feel dirty.'
It was done by sum1 over 30
Watch'n this sort of shit.
Hurts a little bit
Round peg, square holes don't fit.

9/11

Painting a wall in the sun
Looks like there's nowhere 2 run.
Was in the States a year before
Global mural thingy, 29 palms.
Meet some cool artists, open arms.
Stay in touch with a few
Hope 2 c them again anew
I was given the chance on stage.
Words said, now a written page
Not 2 forget the mouse in d cage.
Saw a writer at Venice Beach
Painting a legal wall set up by
Uni students with no provision 4
People wanting 2 learn.
2 paint here u had 2 burn,
Seem 2 b.
We're all connected by c.
This young man
With a can
Had no girl, no job, no plan.
Drugs had hold of this young American
2 find some Adidas shoes 4 gimp
Market stalls. Muscle beach,
Pink man on unicycle, limp whimp,
Same fucking colour as a shrimp,

No one took travellers' cheques.
Past steroid heaven, checks pecs,
2-storey store, graff on d walls.
'Do u take travellers' cheques?'
'Yes!' d 6 ft 4 young negro calls.
Battle of d year video on 3 TVs,
T-shirts with graffiti on sleeves.
Mags on the rack,
From the boys we met way back.
What a strange whack attack
From d land of d Big Mac!
How real is this shit?
Big polite stereotype
In best store in town sell'n hype
While white trailer-park trash
Studied like a rat in cage
4 graffiti crews 2 smash.
Get d cash,
I got d shoes,
U got d news,
Or is it just me views?
Or is it 4 sum1 2 win sum1 has 2 lose?
It has started 2 rain
Our daughter's on a train
The brain, the strain, the pain,
In front of d screen again.
Starting 2 get cold
My arse feels like mould
This story must b told
B 4 we get 2 old.

Jazzi cool

Our daughter was with her gran
While dis work we ran.
Here's what I put in the can:
Jazzi cool, jazzi cool cool, jazzi cool x3
We put u in a pram,
Cool jazzi cool,
While we get caught in a traffic jam.
U stay with nanny Fay
While we work all day,
And when we get home at night
We try 2 get it right.
U jump on Mummy's tit
And Dad says 'Would u like fries
With it?'
Jazzi cool, jazzi cool cool, jazzi cool.
2night 2 men trapped underground
4 5 days have been found
From the land my dad was born.
They were dead
In many people eyes;
5 days with only blackness b4 their eyes.
Time 2 c if the company lies.
U won't give us a chance
2 pull down your pants.

Let's have a dance
With no romance.
I want 2 make a stance
4 u have been blind 4 2 long.
We mustn't prolong
Da wedgey as we pull your thong
Cause u keep doing wrong,
Fuck u ding fucking dong.
The kids smoke d bong
While u have a sing song
4 2 fucking long.
No more national graffiti speak
U r just 2 fucking weak,
Fuck u, freak.
Go & have a leak,
U r speaking 2 d meek
4 we r 2 inherit d earth,
4 all that it's fucking worth.
U seem 2 destroy dis turf
2 make yourself some money,
When bees bring us d honey.
Did u hear what I said, sonny?
U will be left all alone
2 sit on your throne
No 1 2 call on your mobile phone.
Created the lone zone, with a
Drone, prone 2 want 2 live alone.
Seed planted & sown,
Chance created and blown,
Don't think that u r ownin'

'Cause u own,
'Cause u don't,
'Cause u won't.
2 Avski (RIP), sorry, u just came back
2 d memory stack.
It's an old system that I'm using,
Spellcheck is fucking my head.
RIP man, I remember d dead.
Your piece is still on d wall
Cause it was our call,
D shit going down around here.
D wall, now titled @**mass fear**,
Keep writing late in2 da night.
Yeah, I'm ready 2 fight,
2 provide the light,
So some just might
B able 2 help u with your concern.
We need 2 learn
Not every1 must burn.
The world continues 2 turn
So we must b stern.
How old is that fern?
We must sing 2 1 another
Use is this, using is another
Spellcheck in effect.
My daughter does know
If u go with d flow
U will say what u know.
It ain't real smart
2 throw dat dart

With lies & hatred in ur heart.
U may as well just fart
Cause dat ain't art,
It's war.

Our vision of art clubs is easy enough for the writers to understand: safe places to learn and grow as a new culture in a new age. There has been so much change in lifestyle on this dry spot and the whole Western world since the Industrial Revolution. We lead dollar-driven lives, where standards of living stand against quality of life. The tomatoes must be picked. Immigration policies that do not take into account social implications are changing our diversity. Consumers in our democratic zone are blinded by $s and every debate will be won by the biggest pile of $s.

We are not that long out of the trees,
Wearing clothes instead of fleas
Alcohol will keep the workers on their
Knees,
'Honey, have the kids gone 2 Mars in our
Jetcar? I can't find the keys.'
Our $pirit seems to float, misdirected,
On a global warming breeze.
And as much as you try to hide from this
Global mindfuck, please,
Always remember 2 dot your 't's
And cross your 'i's or is it 't's?
Well, well. We need 2 bring on the big gun$.
Yes, we can save u money.

Just in case u didn't hear this
Spellchecked line
That is divine
In the above line
That comes 2 u as a sign
2 decrease what's not fine
In your opinion, not mine.
Which is quiet: clothes line.
We have washed it and hung it on the
Line 2 dry.
Now it's ready 2 try,
Before we all fry
And die
In our wasteland pigsty.
Really bummed out, think I wanna cry,
2 start anew. O=O=O=O=O=O=O=O

Understanding nothing. Yes, this is the beginning. Another day, another holler. Shit, I hate that graffiti shit. Tags on private property. 'What about the pieces?' Well, I do like some of the good stuff. Problem is, you can't have one without the other. Take a seat and let me explain.

A tag is usually a young writer's first step to becoming the above-mentioned appealing artist. Are we addressing their skill development? Answer: No. As some programmes say, they are in place for the whole culture, especially if they are connected to the older writers who in many cases have seen or heard of these programmes that seem to be in place out of kindness instead of care. Well ain't that a nice way to put it? Even after talking to us, some have continued down a path which has had negative effects on these at-risk youth they are employed to care for, all in a kiss-ass way to keep their jobs. Kids end up in the criminal justice system, left to the likes of Salford.

To you, money means more than it should do. This is yet another reminder that forgiving is a way of stopping murders happening. Lucky I don't do too much reading. Eye for an eye is in a book somewhere. Stop hiding from the truth! We cannot continue to programme our youth through the media advertising this culture in their quest for a $. We cannot hide from that fact any longer. Nowhere is this brought up in the media when debate on the issue is raised. Fucking neo-Nazi control freaks. Methinks that needs to be addressed at the highest levels of our controlled lives. Or is it that we have wasted this opportunity of living the last seventeen years, exploring this culture in our quest to make this culture become a part of our community.

No one wants to debate this issue in front of the media with us, yet we are family people with a concern for the future as the sperm and egg have produce a PPE for whom our love is directional, as love can sometimes be. Don't think that all of our love has been soured by freaks, as this would not b written without that stuff in our hearts. Stand up if you have the guts to try and battle against the truth we have come to believe in. That is a better community with less sales based on hate. Fuck was not a word used when we were sold smokes on the TV in the 1970s by the 'Anyhow Have a Whistle' dudes. Now it's 'Fuck those dudes selling smokes'. How time changes! Things are still played out by the masses, and while the masses don't hear from the elders we will continue this hatred in our consumer-driven communities. Please look and listen to what has been written, for to ignore is to allow the whore to destroy our families. 'Peace is for all PPE's; survival is the consequence of creativity!' (Me 2005).

As we are in the same relationships we started seventeen years ago, I must conclude that we have done better than the first youth development officer that we met, who's now in charge of Queensland's first legal brothel. We must tell the story of the quest in two parts so as to not see another young PPE die. We must sing to one another!

I-_-I
lll

with the bits in middle
I need 2 fiddle
2 complete this riddle, we will l8r sk8r.

Cno1.

To say I'm empowered now would be like it. I'm even scaring myself at times. Humble time is needed now. I'm sorry you have demons, Mum. By the way, did Eminem get over that with his vinegar tits Mummy? I'm over it with you, Mum, yet I feel compounded to call the bro in. And no dog shampoo will ever come close to that, eh Al? Yes, I am ready to battle the good. Fight.

As the media sips the nectars of
Suckcess in their war on truth

Our local fish and chip rapper
Has inspired Nats.
Stan is lost somewhere on
Planet pinball.
Stan was last seen in a po-lice uniform
Painting stencils on the M1.
This is just the beginning of Stan the Man
Who got the plan to save the can
Has now been seen in Japan.
You will become a fan of Stan.
There are figures, stats on how
Many people go missing in this

Dry stop (**Australia**) every day, month
Year. Yet we are told 2 live
In fear of those who are still here,
Declaring war on those
Whose message is clear:
Yes, we want 2 paint, not b abducted by
These freaks or left in some kinda
Child restraint.
The message, as written on the chips
And Snapper Wrapper:
'There is nothing wrong with our
Political logic; it's the way we enact it.'

Micheal Franti, *Snapper Wrapper*,
1994ish, employment section.

Graffiti artists 2 paint something.
Phone 666-000-666

Found the duty of care needed to continue this journey. Ring, ring all day. June received no answer. At 9.30 p.m. I tried and was successful and went to see what this new workplace opportunity was about. As luck would have it, a young writer came with us to quote on his first private mural job. On top of the steepest hill in our zone lived the advertisers who were not likely to pick up the baby bonus as sperm and eggs make babies. We were shown the surface of supposed mural that faced downhill across a valley and away from the gay love nest. Both June and I were shunted away as we were not the prey of these horny male lovers looking for something different in their yard/lives. Watching this young writer display his every action, the future employers sized up their prey like a sailor in a brothel. The word was sent out via the underground for all to watch out for this scam. We believe strongly that there were two things that brought on this attempted crime via the snapper wrapper:

1.   the community crackdown on Peter File and his crew;
2.   the influence of a megalomaniac called 'Buffo the Graffiti Slayer'.

As the Peter File crew were running out of places to select their prey from due to more awareness in the community, we noticed some strange bedfellows in need to be places. Buffo had single-handedly managed to use fear in the community to become the saviour of the average redneck short on vision to vent their sexual anger in the direction of the young who seem to be looking for some. It was scary to think the freaks were trying this in our zone. What was even more freaky was that when we reported this strange plot to the po-lice, they fogged us off to the newly appointed children's commissioner in our zone – a fine upstanding stiff in a flash suit with a big office in a big building in the big city. He tried to fog us too, saying that we should talk to a few of his uni buddies as a way of dealing with us. Piss off, was what he really meant, so we did, with yet another one-way dead-end street to add to our road map to nowhere. Trying to bring a better outcome for children being our goal, we still hadn't found the playfield. Sixty-plus-year-old

Salford, the children's commissioner was sacked weeks later for letting his early-twenty-something boyfriend/toyboy/lover loose around the seedy side of town with his government-funded car and credit card.

OK. This is what the world of slime crime is really good at: hiding the shit from the people. We were to run into many more turds on this quest. We couldn't make it without June's family support. Meanwhile, back on the Cold Coast, Buffo, single, fat middle-aged fembot, had seen some writers tagging on their way to the abandoned fun-park where many pieces were done in a relatively safe place for the writers to paint. Buffo then saw the same young man at Pacifier Stair shopping complex and confronted him, who, after being pushed, pushed back so as to defend himself, as one does.

This would turn into his personal crusade to wipe out graffiti. With his slayer senses running out of control and mass snapper-wrapper support for his cause, he was able to convince some, including the justice department, Brisvegas council and po-lice that his wisdom gained from playing good cop and bad cop at that time meant that he could bust every last sucker who ever picked up a can. He had started by buffing tags near his place and spread wider as the media made this slayer an expert overnight, with our proactive stuff still struggling to get trickles of funding. He would soon develop what seemed to be a copy of what we were trying at that time. We went and paid a visit to this slayer, working in what could loosely be termed the same field, to introduce the owners of an underground graff mag. The slayer had his undercover cousin there, and couldn't cut it when questioned by these young writers who owned the mag.

For those who don't know, this interview was published with a warning for writers attached. A $1500 reward for anyone dobbing in a tagger/writer was posted. This set in place the legal painting plan. As this zone we talk of is Australia's number 1 inbound tourist destination, it attracts a lot of young writers from all over Oz. They know that legal walls in the zone are a cool place to meet other writers without fear of the youth workers dogging on them.

So intro: the reformed graffiti writer for Buffo to suck in these interstate visitors in the slayer's lair. The legal paint is where you can meet this reformed god-fearing funky cold redeemer. I still remember her rap about a girl having to keep her tits in her dress or else (**what?**). Sometimes a church minister or preacher, sometimes a drug-fucked skanker, believed it was good to gain the confidence of these PPEs, only to dog them in to Buffo and she could then put the tag to the face and give the po-lice and council what they wanted (**and don't forget the $**). Slow Buffo who was ready to grow a mo, went on to win citizen of the year, running community service programmes that would also get another use out of the youth he had dogged in from his flat for those who were sentenced by the courts to do work in the community. Buffing was usually the task. Buffo's legal approach was worked on with the great justice department, and was basically to disseminate responsibility to local councils if they would do a cost-sharing deal. The pilot proactive programme were the kids chasing the beans and they would front-up at the local po-lice truth centre for six weeks' paintin', at first on boards. Then, when they ran out, it was down to the local shopping place to see how big a cardboard box you could drag back to paint (sounds so satisfying don't it? Not).

Early in this process they had a pro video made to help sell this to the local councils. I still remember Buffo and Dog Girl (Reformed Graffetti Writer) walking passed these painted boards proclaiming their sales: '…and that one's sold, and that one and that one!' etc. We found out that the justice department had bought these boards and that some of the youth, it was said, weren't paid for their works. Due to our work in making those who need to know, know, this scam never went far, even though I have a short footnote about one of the youth who was told to stay away from this programme yet decided he could scam the scammers. He ended up in jail after not being paid for his work and promised so much. He travelled to the coast, (sometimes a four-hour trip) to pick up a payment that never arrived. He became more anti 'The Man'/Slayer, vandalising more than with just a spray can. He smashed a war memorial then went to jail and is now out and dependant on psych drugs to make it through the day. Buffo, where did you go?

On another person's life our paths crossed again. Same result, Buffo. Remember the young Larrykin whose father died under the bus whilst changing a tyre? Came to you for drink-driving community service only for you to have him sign a book, stating he had worked the day when he had just arrived in the morning only for you to send him away, still mourning his father. He drunk some more that day and got busted during the time you had him working for your great cause, Slayer! Well, he did time in jail for this. I still remember his mother's tears on the phone, Slayer! Two males in no time gone from this wife/mother's arms, Slayer! Something you will never know, Slayer! Remember the day before the graff conference in Brizzy when the large mural of the 190 children's faces being painted by us was tagged with words like 'Don't fuck with the lesbians', '666' and other toy-assed shit that was reported to the local press via your fax machine, idiot Slayer! No wonder you had to go, Buffo! 1 km long, 4 m high, four years to complete, two years without funding to which you can claim some credit with your poison pen, even though most of that was done by friends of known offenders against children. So don't ever think you ever won anything, Slayer. By the way, graffiti writers were side by side with us, finishing this mural, Slayer! Why can't you see the pain others have suffered at your greed, Buffo the Graffiti Slayer? Forgiveness is something easier to do if I don't have to see you.

Remember the Australia Day Rewards 2001 when we were nominated for the Olympic torch relay artwork we had painted on over 1,500 power poles in fifteen suburbs across south east Queensland? Images were sent in by students from schools in the region which lay along the relay route. What was your effort for that year? Oh no! Now I remember! You put a private high school on your buffing patrol for a week and, making sure to maximise your public profile, you had these youths in the newspaper, putting them in direct conflict with the taggers. Very smart, idiot Slayer! Do you remember pushing past my sister-in-law who we had to stop from smashing you at this function, Slayer? Just a quick update: that school has worked with myself for the last two years as a part of their community work, painting two murals, one at the Surfers Paradise rowing club, the other at the Surfers Paradise baseball club. Did you know that Xmas is the only time of the year you can say Ho! Ho! Ho! without having three women chase you down the street, Slayer? There's a lot more to tell about this Buffo, but he ain't worth it, are you Buffo?

Is it real, or is it just a dream?

Lazy Grey (successful Australian hip hop MC).

word

Audrey mentioned Di.
June painted her
And I wrote about those who lied.
Word on da street,

Some say,
The paparazzi should never have tried.
Some say
They thrived on attention;
The paparazzi were justified.

Some say
All their trust was with the driver,
On whom they relied.

Some say
The driver's liver was fried
And Dodi & Di died.

Some say
It's a plot to kill the rich, genocide.

Some say
There were speed limits,
They should have complied.

Some say
We knew too much about their lives;
In death we're oversupplied.

Some say
It's been a while now, but for the
Tabloid giants this one qualified
And Dodi & Di died.

Some say
'Did you see the psychic down the
Street, yelling he predicted it?
He seemed so gratified.'

Some say
The monarchy are a plague that
Only needs a little pesticide.

Some say
When it came to a choice between
Charles & Di,
'I was on her side.'

Some say
Why did they live apart?
Why did they divide?
And Dodi & Di died.

Some say
This is a storm in a teacup.
When will this crap subside?

Some say
I'm not down with this shit.
When were the bodies identified?

Some say
There will be questions on people's
Minds for ever.
It's not something
You can just put aside.

Some say
Has anyone thought it might
Have been murder-suicide?
And Dodi & Di died.

Some say
'Why are you so mystified?'
Some say
Was it an act of god?

Some say
God had a shot at someone else;
When he missed he was horrified.

Some say
Well, if your going to cash in your
Chips, France is a nice place to
Collide,
And Dodi & Di died.

Some say
They're not really dead,
Someone has lied.

Some say
The paparazzi were more
Interested in snapping shots before
The blood had dried.

Some say
It's one of those moments when
The world seems to be electrified.
And Dodi & Di died.

Some say
They weren't doing a good
Job if they were trying to hide.

Some say
I don't really give a shit.
Was it their last ride?

Some say
At least they were by each other's side.
Some say
The Royal family should've cried.

Some say
Their fame was short-lived,
Too short, some implied.
And Dodi & Di died.

Some say
I'm getting bored with this,
It's making me tired.

Some say
It would have been much cleaner
If MI5 had used cyanide.

Some say
They were really nice people.
The world was denied.

Some say
I wonder if they were mummified…
And Dodi & Di died.

Some say
What about her poor boys? They
Must have been mortified.

Some say
They were just like Jesus.
Remember? He was crucified.
And Dodi & Di died.

It's strange we have 2 hide.
Sing d kokoda @**massfear** song with pride.
Will moved in next door
Just b4 Bali made a score.
Told him not 2 smile
4 a little while.

He's still next door & his son kicks
Over d fences.
He's allowed 2 cross mine –
That's y we shine
@**mass fear**.

Just lookin' 4 an ear,
Hopin' that it's here.
Sorry dear,
Survive alive,
It's that clear.

My favourite colour.
Don't lie.
Bye
Bye.

Cno1

The Queen's visit

Usually out in the sun
Try'n 2 have some fun
When they blow up 2 towers
Standing in a tunnel for hours
Paint'n parkland flowers
Didn't get wet in d showers
For the right 2 'ave a say
Sumtimes there's a price u 'ave 2 pay
2 live this way
CHOGM was only days away.
On the day
D Queen was 2 open d park
D world was wait'n 4 d next spark
& we r paint'n under the mainline
Where d sun don't shine
One hell of a target
It's not easy 2 forget
Finished with no regret
Ball hit the cord, dat's a let
Not far from d children's
Commissioner's office! Tag it!
CHOGM was moved 2 chaddy shack
2 avoid attack.
Queen drove past the mural slow
Cops everywhere, photos 2 show.
Park was opened by the Queen
Not a bomber 2 b seen
The grass was so green.

I'm a Republican,
Don't want 2 b lead
By sum1 who can bury dere head.
D French let off bombs in d Pacific
Not in the English Channel specific
An English tourist icon, how terrific!
Don't get me wrong
English footy's got its own song
Commonwealth, common health
Head of state, (who's ya mate?)
I was only 20-1 = 19
OK, d suicide bomber saw it dis way
4 dat day d family stay'd away
D photo I took
Should b in d book.

There seems to be much talk about how to bring our community together with religious divisions and wars overseas that have proven that everyone cooks their peas differently. So where does this uniting come from? Is it the soccer World Cup that will have a uniting effect on those many new Aussies who in the stands were finally yelling 'Ozzie Aussie Orzy!' for the first time in their lives. 'Thank God for that goal. As it seems to me that it helped this group of new Aussies get a common goal for all to unite. This was something I took great interest in as many of these new Aussies in the stands have never been given a chance to celebrate a sporting victory in the sport they are following. This moment was one that was of major benefit to our nation as prior to this the game nationally was scarred by violence between ethnic groups, who now have a nation to cheer for. Good for some, yet not for all, as not everyone has the world game as their uniting force in their lives. It's hard to teach an old wombat new tricks.

What we have to offer is a small shift in a culture that could provide this much-needed unity in the community. How about that? We want to put the unity in community. Hip hop, you can't stop, so why not look behind the writing on the wall and ask us any questions you like about our vision for a better future. We have some answers that might just stop those idiots in the media from declaring war on our own and provide a chance for differences at religious levels to take a back seat in the art clubs we are trying to get up and running in the zones as we have suggested. This is the way of truly connecting this international subculture to the mainstream.

Nowhere do we see the mind programming of the marketeers selling their products in this debate thus far, except maybe one interview I did on the ABC radio in Brisbane recently, where the DJ was asking the new minister of defence for our federal parliament on their qualifications. What? Minister for defence one week and minister for moo cow the next? Wisdom at the wave of a vote? You're kidding!

We must sing to one another before we have another case of mistaken identity on this planet. This is one of our greatest concerns and a driving force that pushes us on through the darkness of the political empire-builders that clutter the halls of our lives in this not quite perfect world we call home. Mistaken identity is what happened when a young man was shot by the po-lice in England just after the underground bombs went off in the copycat behaviour that has happened around the Western world since 11 September 2001.

We are now in the new age
Of anti-rage,
As the downtrodden feel the
Need 2 escape their cage
& head 4 a new stage.

70 virgins r offered, it's true
Some 1 wrote it on a page.
Look, it's happening somewhere
Else, time 2 engage.
Or is it time 2 plant sage,
Just trying 2 earn a wage.
If we r 2 c u r us, then we must
Sing 2 1 another,
4 we must recover
From the smother.
We have just blown our cover
That makes us less of a lover.
In the quest 4 the best
We have forgotten the test
That will make us forget the
Pest
That lives in our nest
While plotting against the
Rest.
Straps on a vest
2 blow up those who survive
On their zest.
Have we forgotten our voice?
'Cause when given the choice
We vote 4 those who admit 2
Lying
And cheating
So are we just bleating,
From our central heating
We give this greeting?

Our concern seems fleeting.
Or is it time 2 give and receive
A beating.
While the world it is that we
Are defeating?

Have you ever seen a graffiti writer painting in a train yard with cameras that want to find out their identity? Yes, they do look like Muslim women with their faces all covered up except for their eyes and they will usually have a backpack that could be mistaken as a bomb. Mistaken identity meant that some po-lice person shot the dentist's son, thinking he was a terrorist. Sort of 'friendly fire', the USA would call it, as they do when they kill their own in the name of God. Hopefully we won't come to this or the shot will miss (isn't that the way we refer to unmarried females when they are young?)

As the left & right of
Our political systems
Jockey 4 the vote,
We somewhat feel remote,
As our belief is somewhat
Stuck in a moat,
Not even a boat.
Somehow we feel like the
Undercoat.
Looking for a way to float.
Being chased around the
Propane BBQ by a two-headed
Goat.
Who's wearing a $uperman
Coat.

Whilst looking 4 another way
2 bloat.
Or is it a need 2 lie & cheat
Then gloat?
It is 4 this reason our lives we
Do devote.
4 the community acceptance
Of hip hop (as appeared in the same
Fish & chip
Wrapper that declared war on graffiti last
Week. It states in the headline:
'Aussie tracksuits 2 b hip hop
Tracksuits' in yesterday's
Dribble – the Melbourne Herald-Sin.)
In our communities is
What we promote!

For the kids as parents we love, as PPEs we love. Our land has had the influence of money on it for less time than most of the rest of the planet and when you take your shoes off you can feel it. It's real, just like them fridge magnets. We must sing to one another.

A few days have passed since I last hit the board. The Herald-Sin his done it again with the headline: WAR ON GRAFFITI HAS AFFECTED THE FIGHT ON DRUGS. It seems that some fuckwit with the vote of the people behind them has made a mistake again, taken po-lice from the drug squad to fight this war against an enemy that has only ever killed itself. Drugs you don't see; graffiti you do. And thank fuck for that, otherwise we might never have exposed this short-sighted, ego-driven idiot who should be asked the question, 'who's da crim?' More drugs? Let's make that a political policy. This is not what I wanna be doing with our voice, yet it seems to be the only way to make this concern in our communities have a voice. With a couple of days away from this screen to talk to the bloke on the street about our theory, which involves just a little shift in a positive direction to make a big difference, it reminds me of the hope that has me here now, that one day this may be out there for those who are concerned about our future, so that they may have a look at what we have seen.

Our local zone head council has called for all the councils to come together without inviting us to the table, so June called the various players in this zone.

She found out that they all have issues with one another and it is unlikely that they will be able to come to some sort of arrangement that could be the answer to their concern. As the state has circumscribed their solutions policy they see this as a funding grab that they can dominate. The biggest council in our zone are using their muscle to grab at what they see as some hope. They can paint everything almond, beige or grey! Children who are drawn to this culture are not murderers, thieves, rapists, terrorists, Peter Files, arsonists or footballers; they are just our kids. Declaring war on them via the media kills them. I'm sad about this and now challenge them dollar-driven fuckers to stand up to me anywhere, any time, for I got something to say, aaaaahhh!

While we continue to push even our own away, we fight in other lands, saying we know better. This is not right. Read this back and you will find that it all started with a wack attack from the land of the Big Mac (**please note: no spellcheck on the word humburger**) Who controls the cashews? Nuts to feed us, or is it nuts to write this?

'**It's S Mac time!**' Now that's what everyone around the world keeps saying. We mustn't stop lookin' at small pictures while the big one is out there.

Stand up you half-steppers
with your Dr Peppers,
the time comes
when we need to eat.
Are you ready for defeat?

Cal I-_-I
lll

Editor found this. The truth is easy to remember ×2:

10-11 changed the theme of the wall
It's 4 world peace we call.
Local newspooper
Has front paged this blooper,
The world's in a stupor,
This was a day to remember,
1 month after 11 september.
4 stand'n on d said wall
I received the mobile call.
Po-lice raid searched every hall.
Strange feelin'
When your play'n cards & u don't
Know who's dealing
The local fed member knew I
Was not happy.
Baby girl's there wear'n a nappy.
4 women & a baby, really crappy,
We had an open day 4 people 2 sign
On the scrolls of peace as part-
Revamped design.

Preachers, teachers, students,
Pollies, war widows; all signed,
Design fine. Time 4 some wine.

14 February 2006

Last time I wrote some stuff about a little something like this, I had already given the roses, roses. Today I tried to help a family member, only to expose another's demons. Bitter-sweet kind of a day. Hope they see that my heart is… We went to see super dude po-lice at Bogan Central, a 6 ft 6, 140 kg teddy bear with a big desk. June and I spoke of our work, some of which he had already seen or heard of. He spoke of the direction he gave to his staff to paint over some tags with their special weapon, the B tag stencil, once and for all proving that two wrongs don't make a right, three lefts do. It wasn't until we explained to the big unit our quest to create clubs and the projected benefits and target zone and better, smarter stuff than what's happening now,

> Was he able to see that he
> Had just been put over the knee
> Spanked a little then set free,
> This man who's as big as a tree.

(**Saw old Ted there too.**) Hope this was all good. Methinks spill cheque do nut in. Yew 'ave 2 lock ad id.

We don't want to see another raid here like the one that was a part of the scared weird big guys running around with their heads in a spin after 11-9-1 / 9-11-1. It was on 10-October when a mural we were working on at the time with a CJP programme was print media front page colour photo with the section of this main road overpass mural showing a hippie chic sitting down, leaning towards her sign board that read, MAKE LOVE NOT WAR. Props, Tammy. And of course, as history and the Simpsons would have it, something bringing love should have its legs broken.

Standing at the end of the street with a STOP/GO sign, I was angry after a phone call from June to tell me about a po-lice raid on our home office. Practically the whole family had been present when it happened: the mother-in-law, daughter, June and staff Jacque (**the keeper of official secrets. well, she had a baby on a Sunday, after working on a scaffold the previous Friday with nine** months of playing 'hide the bump'. She was only found out when her mum, dad and brother came to the door on the Sunday morning, expressing some concern about her.

'Did you hear about Jacque?' they said at the front door, early that sleep-in morning. I expected some horror story, but they went on to say she had had a son; to which my reply was, 'There goes the theory she's a lesbian.' Ha ha! Laughter was heard. Love to them).

> I rang the local federal member and
> Told them our door is open,
> Why don't they see that?
> Welcome sign on the door mat,
> Even to the fat cat from the land of the
> Big Mac where people smoke
> Crack & shoot smack to get a wack
> Attack whilst playing 'My
> Sherona' by 'The Knack'. Or is it love
> They lack?

Well how about that? On the top of the terror list! Boo isn't spelt with a 'p', shitheads. Well, well. Four years on we film *The Kokoda Challenge* on the Gold Coast, a fund-raising bush walk so youth could see what the world was like sixty years ago. Sleepless night as the first team finished at 2.30 a.m. Got a bunch of film on this great event. It had to be edited within a week for the governor general of Australia to see at the official dinner and presentation. June and I were guests. I took the camera and was not fun for June to be with, standing with the honour guard with a camera in my hand, inches from the G/G. I ask the very same federal who couldn't tell us why we were raided if she thought that maybe we had just been taken off the list of terrorists planning to kill things. Why are PPEs so…?

On 11 October 2002 – that's right, one month after September 11 – we had a po-lice raid on our home, just after 9 a.m. We were in the local paper on the front page with a colour photo of a mural we were painting on the Centenary of Federation here in Oz. September 11 happened and we added some to this piece, with a peace theme that appear on the front page: MAKE LOVE NOT WAR was the message. Women were in black. There was my daughter, June, June's mum and a staffer female in the house at the time, ringing me on-site about the raid. I rang the local federal member and made suggestions about coming for a BBQ, a cup of tea or whatever as our door is always open. In this moment of disbelief

I think I said something about not pissing me off as these one-shot kamikazes would be the least of their worries. And if you are reading this now… Well, do I have to say any more? Yes I do, as the same freaks who allowed this home invasion to happen also let me loose in front of the Governor General of Australia last year, 2005, with a movie camera, standing within inches of what seems to be a nice bloke. Of course I had to ask the local federal member whether or not we were off the terrorist list, which we're sure to be back on if someone has the balls to publish this.

As this bloke did say
In his speech 2day
There's a price u 'ave 2 pay
For not giving our youth
Somewhere 2 play.
Rang him, he had nothing. Touché.
Wisdom power – de power, the Queen.
Sorry, it's not your fault u
Were born as it is not mine.
All that is, is just fine.
Ha like ha Grandma.
They found dinosaurs in de tar.
Gotta flick of u in d car.
Passing one of our murals under
The train line. Everything is fine.

Today we had a print media story in the Sunday Mail, with June questioning the funds being spent, and an editorial comment that made us look like we are trying to support the rednecks who don't see the marketing forces that programme the minds of our youth. The editorial said that all graffiti is bad and should be terminated. Well, well. That's the power of the press and if this has done one thing it has created a platform for debate. Let's hope it's with the media present as they take much joy in beating up on this subject. The empire-builders in their glass houses have much to be concerned about, if they want to battle. It would be in my opinion a bit like playing football with the blind and taking the bell out of the ball. (No, we are not in the planning stages of doing a mural for the Guide Dogs' Association. We are gonna do it, no offence to those who must see without their eyes.)

There was a TV story last night about the road toll, with some much-learned surgeons speaking on the subject of risk taken by the (mainly male) minds of the under twenty-five-year olds and the influence of the media. If only we were surgeons, then our opinion might be worth something. Oh well. Seventeen years studying graffiti seems like a waste of time. Or is it? Stand up, Mr & Mrs Decision Makers and debate this matter with those who have done this, instead of having national conferences with Prof. Tosser getting up to explain the workings of a child's mind based on the photo of some graffiti in the local hood he had taken the day before. I then stood up and called him a wanker as this graffiti was painted by someone who runs their own business and is over thirty. I had to watch the public servants treat this national summit as a holiday, as we watch our young being programmed by the media these fuckers live by. 'Sell' rhymes with 'hell' for a good reason. I watch one council try to sell their failing programme to another who's trying the same number on them. Then there's the dinner where casual sex seems to be more important than the subject matter at hand. Why? Because the dinner is outside work hours. So is the graffiti, dumb fucks. You can't see 'cause you are not looking at anything but yourself. Why are the people in the factories paying you to do this? Why are the people overseeing you allowing this to happen? Why is it that we can see this and feel pain when many shut their minds to this concern and hope that this sort of process will fix it? Bring me the greatest minds in the land – no, the world – and let's discuss the concern of graffiti on this, the third rock from the sun which we call Earth. This can happen. I've got a backyard and a BBQ, just come on round! That reminds me, I said those words before. Took a grab, 2005 grand final. One grab, 2006.

April Fool

Flew to Sydney a couple of weeks ago to see what the Americans were up to with the new Homeland Security Department. That's right, it was April Fool's Day 2006. With our new Free Trade Agreement, the Yanks are looking for better ways of feeling safe in the hood. Had to get up at 3.30 a.m. to get to the airport for an early flight so as to compensate for the hour's time difference due to daylight saving in New South Wales. Arriving at the airport on time, I was still half asleep. Walking through the gate lounges, I noticed a sign that had graffiti sprayed over it and spray cans left on top of it. This is more than just an ad. It's a statement of defeat. Who's allowing this to be there for all to see?

At one time in my life you wouldn't hear swearing on TV, yet they would sell you smoke. Now I'll have to kill the next fucker trying to sell smokes to the kids is going to become our next reality TV show. Brought to you by Planet Petrol.

Meanwhile on the 44th floor of the high-rise overlooking Sydney Harbour, it's 8.30 a.m. as the lift door opens to the Homeland Security conference. And I'm there on time being questioned as to whether or not I was in the right place. My name tag had to be written on the spot even though I was booked to be there. With my hair tied above my head as is my custom and a suit jacket on as is not, I listened to what was an explanation of how twenty-two departments merged to become Homeland Security. They were a little lost as to what it all meant, methinks. Listening to what they had to say I was quite shocked to find they didn't have any idea how many illegal aliens were in da USA. Nor did they have a system in place to stop people getting a driver's licence in different states.

These illegal aliens seem to be
The replacements for the slaves
Of the old USA:
Happy to get any pay,
Shut up, scream into the pillow
Or they won't let us stay.
Is this the right way?
The government turns a blind eye
2 the cheap workers who r not gay
And will have children 1 day.

charlie chaplin

Commercialism. Now that's a big word.
Fight where kids could get hurt.
Yeah, there, care, stare if u dare. I was there.
So I did for the sake of the kid, I did.
What a strange way 2 b when u are 44.
Did some1 forget 2 produce a floor?
Oh no! I'm falling again into now and zen.
Is that a big number as I go 4 my slumber?
What a strange bunch of words I have
Written. So there is a reason 4 da words
As they help me remember events in my
Kind mind. I find it is time to finish what
Has been started on Australia Day.
Much has happened since the time in this
Seat when the rest was penned. I've had
Another look at the local hood, trying
2 find good, if only I could, I would, now
It's back 2 da what I know I should,
'Cause it's all fucking good.
Self, wealth, health, stealth and
Concern 4 da ina elf. Some1 said life is a
Shit sandwich. The more bread u got the
Less shit u gotta eat. Now don't that
Make our lives complete? It's time 2 get 2
Me feet. Now I'm forcing myself 2
Compete from this fucking seat.

Stand up if you're sick of the corrupt.
Stand up if children are being fucked.

They r gonna want 2 stay.
Find an identity and pray.
Hopefully 2 da 1 god and don't stray. 4
The experts would b calling in the army
As these aliens have the profile of a
Copycat terrorist they'd say. Touché.

Now back to the 44th floor, Sydney, April Fool's Day. The speeches from the players seemed to be leading the techno way: border security, new ways of detecting the illegal aliens, systems to be found to stop the duplication of identity between states and the way to use a PC to stop this problem. They explained they didn't know what they were looking for if a concern wasn't raised. So as it is our concern to bring the culture of hip hop out from the darkness of the underground, I allowed a couple of questions from the floor before I asked if they were into social programmes that would help bring some unity to their community. To my surprise, I wasn't thrown from the 44th floor or even shown the door, even though there was a pause before the appointed member of team USA replied. He said that this sort of approach could be considered and conceded that it was a good idea.

Swap some cards and made my way clear,
4 44 floors up Homeland Security terror
Fear. Did I make myself clear? I'm glad
They were there 2 hear, now off to c
Daddy dear, cause he lives very near.
As I left the next day I shed a tear.
Headlines in the newspoopers have
Bikies shooting, stabbing and jabbing at
A kickboxing tournament. Young
Drivers going 2 fast and killing
Innocents. Street fights leading 2
Deaths, 2 in this year near local pubs,
One of which took the life of an old
Teammate's son. Ain't life some much
Fun? My family's been so sick, hope the
Chemo does the trick. Praying that we
Can soon give this shit the flick. Life's a

Game that can be over in one kick. Ice is the
Drug this idiot was on, when he cut off
His balls with 1 nick, silly prick, should
Have gone the whole hog and cut off his
Dick. There's been fuck all good news
Since the visit from St Nic.

As the newspoopers call for answers to youth driving too fast, on page three they place a girl in her skin-tight swimsuit. Shout out to the Indy race later in the year, the message I sent was clear, that shouting out to speed is our fear. Why don't we get the smoking message into other areas of this sadomasochistic society? Maybe if the life of a newspooper editor's child was to be taken they may look beyond their wallet to address the real cause of what influenced this need for speed or greed.

Oh, it's Easter again, time to give the hungry a feed.
That should make it all better.
Front page, yes, indeed.
Eat lots of chocolate and make crops that don't seed.
Hide behind your $ u fucking weed.
Who put the sup into
Press? What a disgraceful mess. If 0 was
The lowest, u would b worth less.
U really don't give a fuck, confess.
There's shit out there u don't and won't address.
With our need 2 seek the truth, blinded
By the $. We seem 2 have thrown away the
Moral collar. So much do we love the $.

We will vote in a liar to lead us as financial security wins the election. Is the truth worth 0? Is this the message we want to leave our children – moral infection section in the library of bribery? Now is the time to develop the creative minds so we can evolve beyond this commercial that is playing games with our species. Community can be provided by the art clubs we are gonna create.

The people in the street
Can understand that this
Would help keep us all on our feet.

Our community has an answer
That is gonna work a treat.
All the naysayers
Should get ready for defeat.

Went 2 da footie with me daughter. Brizzy Lions v. Essendon bombers AFL. As for understanding club street, these two AFL clubs are a part of a national code and turn over millions of $. There are other codes of footie that are more international and compete in global comps, lawnbowls, tennis, netball, squash, sailing, surfing, basketball, diving, swimming, high jump, long jump… I think you get the picture. It's from the one breath that all these pastimes came into being.

I had been doing a legal (painting graffiti on a legal site is as rare as rabbits laying eggs) for most of the day. I rushed home, picked up me girl and off we went to the footie. She was there as part of a junior development programme called Auskick. Kids under ten play a no-contact version of the big boys' game. We went into the gabba and watched the teams warming up and kicking goals. That's when Dad took a grab-a. I took a few photos, watched the first quarter, then we went off to the changing rooms so the kids could get ready to make a debut in front of 30,000 or more fans. Somehow I was asked to do the goal umpiring, which gave me a chance to be close to me girl (mini-me in drag). The siren blew for half-time and out ran the kids, about 100 of them to be playing in separate parts of the field, with the zone allocated for our kids just in front of the players' race (entry? exit? tunnel?).

I was carrying plastic goal post and flags, wearing what could only be described as a goal umpire's jacket that was two sizes too small. Trying to hold everything on this humid playing surface under lights, I notice the big boys of the AFL had decided not to leave the field after the siren as they wanted to have a bit of push and shove, which with my knowledge of the game can spread quickly. Without a second thought, I waddle myself into a place between the kids and the big boys. Looking back briefly to make sure all the kids were behind me, a strange feeling came over me as if I was in the movie *Invasion of the Body Snatchers*. There was not one other parent, coach or adult who put themselves in position to protect the kids. 30,000 or more in the stands, 100 kids on half the field, thirty-six players in agro mode on the other half, and one proud dad in the middle.

The players left for their half-time break and the kids played their game. The siren went, the kids started to run around the boundary, getting pats on the back and low fives from the crowd, just as the Lions come through the race. Me goal posts went to the turf as again I put myself between the kids and the potential accident coming their way. The team entered and the kids went to the changing rooms safely.

The Lions won.

> Me girl said, 'Dad, that was the best
> Time I've ever had,'
> So now I'm a glad, mad dad who
> Gave it all he had and took a grab(@dagabba).
> Since 1989 we have had many times
> When we have had 2 put ourselves
> Between the truth and the crimes.
> Politics and da media r 1 & the same,
> Always looking 4 sum1 2 blame,
> Lying & cheating, it brings on da shame,
> You're just so fucking nowhere, you're lame.
> Turn off the bullshit & play the 1 game.
> Just hand me the baby, take a photo man
> I just gotta find a plan.
> Just get rid of the spray can.
> Night-time curfew? Yeah, we'll place a ban,
> Just hand me the baby, take a flick quick,
> I'm on a time line 2 suck, lick da mans dick
> What, u thought my job's a prick picnic?
> Well u r right, it is, 'cause I suck.
> And if you're looking 4 help u r outta luck,
> When it comes 2 your concerns I don't
> Give a fuck.
>
> Take back this baby, it's shit, fuck muck.
> Thank u, thank u, thank u we'll do lunch.
> Our leaders double as bottom feeders.

2000

When I write,
I try not 2 bite.
Vision from a private satellite
Shining like a beacon
2 try & stop the freak'n
U know the boat is leak'n?
Our strength sum try 2 weak'n,
By lying, cheat'n, sneak'n.
On a planet full of war & hate
Just grab a date,
No matter which state,
Strength comes have'n a mate.
The school of hard knocks
Is were this culture rocks,
Not 2 many writers wear frocks
Or worry about golden locks
Or socks in d jocks down d docks.
Remembering Bondi
Legal on the beach only 2 die
Sum1 likes it, sum1 don't
1minute we'll allow it
D next we won't.
U make decisions dat seem 2 burn.
What did u learn?

Or is it earn
D smoke clears which way 2 turn
Photo op, I'm plant'n a fern.
Graffiti is no longer my concern,
Writers would make great pollies,
Kiss'n babies, hand'n out lollies
Not! Even though
They sometimes look through da
Same window.
We all gotta seed 2 sow.
Wait, I'll just go blow, snow,
Below, u know, Jo So & So Flow,
Doing raps with kids
Lift'n their lids.
Sum would luv 2 b writers
And not just 1 nighters.
What can we provide?
Sumwhere 2 hide?
4 without our plan
& de help of da man
They r gonna put u in da can.
Graffiti is older than Jesus
Used in ads 2 please us
As we brainwash da youth
The man hides from de truth
Open your eyes, u'll see da proof.
U r there 2 work 4 us, not goof.
Don't turn away, act aloof
We need your decision
Kids r dying due 2 lack of vision.

We r kill'n our own,
Gangsta shit on d mobile phone,
Now that our cover is blown,
U know we r not alone.
We ain't about creatin' a clone
Looking outside the zone,
Describing d way we're prone.
Can't wait 2 c an election
Text message defection
Face'n rejection
Consumer infection;
At the push of a button,
Lamb turned into mutton.
Did u c the swing in de safe sea?
Shit we're facin' defeat.
Look up and listen,
It ain't all about baby kissin'.
Have concern 4 all de classes,
It might mean kiss'n sum asses.
Put on your glasses,
Let's look after de masses,
4 dae is @mass fear,
Did I make this clear?
It's me favourite colour.
So now is the time 4 sum1
2 help champion this cause,
No need 4 applause,
Just some keys 2 de doors
Access 2 the upper floors
Art clubs r as much ours as urs
Remember June's work at scores?

Financial freedom.
=
Underground
=
Drugs
=
Loose
=
Loose
=
Who's da boss?
=
Confusion
=
Delusion
=
Passion
=
Art
=
Start
=
Life
=
Strife
=
Conflict
=
Anger
=
Danger
=
Stranger
=
System
=
2

=

Love

=

Children

=

Pen

=

Paper

=

Maths

=

Numbers

=

Feed

=

Need

=

Greed

=

Hunger

=

Want

=

Font

=

Culture

=

Difference

=

Defence

=

Fence

=

Separation

=

Nation

=

Station
=
Railway
=
Transport
=
Resort
=
Port
=
Sort
=
Naught
=
Thought
=
Condom
=
Thong
=
Ass
=
Glass
=
Pass
=
Through
=
Drew
=
Jew
=
You
=
Few
=
Stew

=
Do
=
Poo
=
New
=
Spew
=
Chuck
=
Luck
=
Fuck
=
Truck
=
Duck
=
Muck
=
Graffiti
=
Freedom.

Perfect effect, no defect.
We employ writers.
They're some who try 2 bite us,
Only 2 find faults in d plan.
U change d law as only u can,
Made a drain legal
Then went 2 study the mating
Habits of da bald beagle.
Dog that is.
What da fuck u doing in d biz?
It would b cool if you were Liz.
But u ain't,
U need a restraint,
4 what u did made people faint
& it wasn't from d paint
& didn't show 1/4 of my complaint.
'Hey, Dad? U know how u said when it's
Legal, I can do graffiti?
The council says it's OK.
They have drains 2 spray.'
'All right, son. Take ur sister to play,
I can watch da footy 2day.'
With no duty of care,
The kids were stripped bare,
Was only so much room there.
Black eyes from which 2 stare,
'Twas a father's nightmare.
How dare da Mayor
Allow such a liar?
Did they really care?

We had tried 2 say
U r going de wrong way
And now there is a price 2 pay.
5 young writers spoke 2 me
Ask'n what did I c:
Young writers started legally
Now find nowhere 2 b.
Well done, 5x a fork in da road
From da land of da cane toad.
Who's da crim? Dimsimjim?
What? Who's graffiti…

Well, today we saw the most amazing piece of graffiti. Some inspired earthworm walked along the front of a mural we are working on to express their concern that a white ant-infested tree had been felled before it fell on an innocent on a major road. The theme of the mural was to show how few of these trees were left. We must sing to one another.

Ask d **?** – d mark
U dumb fucker, still
In da dark.
Very dark green!
U r now into graffiti
R u ready 2 battle?
And we still wonder y,
If we is born,we is gonna die.
Get over it
U fucking shit
Now back 2 the **?**, d mark
What's de profile of a writer?

In my opinion, just like a surfy.
One's a CEO and one's a hippy,
Send me the psych
& I'll put 'em on dere bike.
Just hand me de mike,
Me tinks Buffo was a dyke.
If u r down 4 da cause,
U hang around 4 da applause.
We don't have 2 change da laws,
If u would stop pick'n ur sores
And accept dat dere yours.
That's da kids I'm talking about,
Brainwashed 2 drink d stout.
Da media has some clout,
Fuck'n money is what made de lout
Give this cause some, 2 bail us out.
U'll never know what u might find
In a young creative mind.
See number one –
Da greatest graffiti I ever saw
On a condom vending machine:
'4 refund insert baby.'
2day 2 gold miners were freed,
2 weeks underground, they didn't need.
Give de hungry a feed.

We need to stop this half-stepper shit and fund the smart art clubs now or leave our youth underground for life. It's simple for the readers of this book: look at one website – **artcrimes.com**. There you will find the **?**, the mark. Idiots who don't use what is there for all to see are fucking with our children's lives yet they don't call themselves Peter Files, they call themselves political leaders.

Fuck me! I ain't got much more (**Michael**)
Left to say,
It's the 2nd Sunday
In the month of May
Mother's Day.

On the same day they rescued the two surviving miners from the earth, three blokes were found lost at sea for twenty-two days. The media again burying their heads to ignore what there was to see. **RIP**.

June's painting a mural for the children's room in a women's prison. We must sing to one another:

That reminds me, vagina
It rhymes with gold miner.
I think I'm going insane,
I think I've lost my mind.
If the answer is what
I'm looking for,
Why is it that questions
Are all I find?
There are so many things to do,
New curtains, carpets, tiles.
Life is such an abyss.
You say you're looking for
The answer.
I say, you don't know what
The question is!
Let's take it back to the

Start.
Sitting on my granddaddy's
Knee, life was simple.
My butt and my face were
Brothers then,
Great big dimples.
I remember him saying as I
Reached for some pie,
'Life taught me something
Boy, that is
If you don't eat,
You don't shit,
If you don't shit, you die.'
1965: Jack.

1992: me.
Climbed that mountain,
Sat on top.
Now you've come this far,
Why cant you stop?
Living in time when the
Truth is a lie,
Why are there so many
Children who want to die?
You tell us a pile of shit
To get our vote,
Then you move to a castle
And build a moat.
…Fun.
Stan from Melbourne
Came 2 life as an international

...Manhunt
Was launch 4 dis graffiti cunt.
This might b a little blunt
4 we tell d story of d media stunt
Performed by a runt 4 money.
Chopper –
Me missus sent u a message,
Me daughter won $20 diss'n u
In d poetry slam at Byron,
'Cos she likes Joel Turner.
Me bro-in-law's in Woodford.
Me soul's in crisis
From female devices.
And you r now a rapper.
This is some of a book
4 u 2 'ave a look.
Hope it don't make u crook.
We must sing 2 1 another,
Just treat me like a brother.
So if I'm dying of a heart
Attack in d South,
Don't give me mouth 2 mouth.
Bartender does the 1/2 stepper
Want a Dr Pepper?
Played in 5 Aussie rules grand
Finals.
Still alive.
Had a thought 2day.
There was God,
The thinker and the devil.

One was an angel,
One was an arsehole,
The one in d middle was a drinker.
Cheers no ears!
Kookaburra lying dead on the
Side of d road,
Hit by a semi, carrying a load
Laugh now, u little mother-
Fucker
While the dog sits on d box full
Of tucker.
Did a gig and finished with the
Word 'vagina';
Wasn't till later that I
Thought it rhymed wit'
'Gold miner'.
U have now seen a little of
What we have.
Buy me a beer
And we can talk some shit;
Maybe we can change a little
Bit.

I-_-I
lll

Peace 441961

From: Phantast
Sent: Monday, May 08, 2006 9:38 p.m.
Subject: re: another great story

Hi Art & Uncle Bill,

This is just some of the mission. Had a strange day, thought I had a vision of God, the thinker & the Devil. One was an angel, one was the an arsehole, the other was a drinker – cheers!

At New York's Kennedy Airport today, an individual later discovered to be a public school teacher was arrested trying to board a flight while in possession of a ruler, a protractor, a setsquare, a slide rule, and a calculator. At a morning press conference, the Attorney General said he believes the man is a member of the notorious Al-gebra movement. He is being charged by the FBI with carrying Weapons of Math Instruction.

'Al-gebra is a fearsome cult,' a Justice Department spokesman said. 'They desire average solutions by means and extremes, and sometimes go off on tangents in a search of absolute value. They use secret code names like 'x' and 'y' and refer to themselves as 'unknowns', but we have determined they belong to a common denominator of the axis of evil with coordinates in every country. As the Greek philanderer Isosceles used to say, 'there are three sides to every triangle.'

When asked to comment on the arrest, President Bush said, 'If God had wanted us to have better weapons of Math Instruction, he would have given us more fingers and toes.'

No virus found in this incoming message.

www.ingramcontent.com/pod-product-compliance
Lightning Source LLC
Chambersburg PA
CBHW081727220526
45468CB00008B/2004